Anonymous

The Hatfield Cook Book

Plain and fancy recipes

Anonymous

The Hatfield Cook Book
Plain and fancy recipes

ISBN/EAN: 9783744781350

Printed in Europe, USA, Canada, Australia, Japan

Cover: Foto ©Lupo / pixelio.de

More available books at **www.hansebooks.com**

The Hatfield Cook Book.

PLAIN AND FANCY RECIPES,

ARRANGED BY

THE "REAL FOLKS"

OF

THE CONGREGATIONAL CHURCH,

HATFIELD, MASS.

HOLYOKE, MASS.,
HUBBARD & TABER PRINTING CO.
1899.

REMARKS.

THE HATFIELD COOK BOOK is sent forth to the public with best wishes to all patrons for its success. The Recipes given are "tested" ones. This means more to good housekeepers than words alone. May each housewife or maiden who attempts a recipe reap success to her personal efforts, and remember that tact and common sense are as necessary in cooking, as in many other practical duties of life.

SOUPS.

"Who builds the fire for his wife, much happiness will find in life."

TOMATO SOUP.

Two quarts of cold water, eight large tomatoes, four rolled crackers, pepper and salt. When nearly done, put in a piece of butter the size of an egg, one teaspoon of soda dissolved in one cup of milk, put in just as you take it off the fire.

MRS. M. N. HUBBARD.

TOMATO SOUP.

One can tomatoes, one pint water; boil hard until tomato is cooked. Add one-fourth teaspoon soda, strain, set on stove and season with butter, salt and pepper. Add slowly one pint of milk, and let come to a boil

MRS. J. E. PORTER.

TOMATO BISQUE.

Three pints milk boiled in double boiler, one can tomato soup (condensed.) The tomato is to be added to soup just before serving. One tablespoon of flour improves the soup.

MRS. R. M. WOODS.

VEGETABLE SOUP.

Two quarts clear stock, skimmed clean of every particle of fat, one carrot, one onion, one potato, one-half cup rice. Cook carrot, onion and potato in a part of stock until tender. Add rice and cooked vegetables to remainder of stock and cook half an hour before serving.

MRS. R. M. WOODS.

POTATO SOUP.

Three potatoes, one teaspoon chopped onions, one teaspoon salt, one-half tablespoon butter, one-half tablespoon flour, one pint of milk. Cook potatoes until soft and mash. Cook onions in the milk and add to the potato, strain. Cook flour and butter together, add to the other and cook five minutes.

MRS. HENRY A. WARNER.

CHICKEN SOUP.

Three or four pounds of fowl. Three quarts cold water, one tablespoon salt, one tablespoon chopped onions, two tablespoons chopped celery. one pint of cream, one tablespoon butter, one tablespoon corn starch, one teaspoon salt, one salt spoon white pepper, two eggs.

MRS. GEORGE A. BILLINGS.

MOCK TURTLE SOUP.

Boil one pound of calf's liver and two pounds of veal two hours, skimming well, then strain, chop the meat fine and add to it a small onion chopped. Salt, pepper and ground cloves to taste, thickening all with a tablespoonful of browned flour, and boiling all up together. Have four hard boiled eggs, cut up in tureen, also one lemon sliced.

MRS. C. E. HUBBARD.

CHICKEN SOUP.

Set the liquor in which two or three fowls have been boiled, away to cool. Skim off the fat, and then put it into the soup kettle, with one whole onion and a half cup of rice; boil two hours. Just before dishing, take out onion and put in some pieces of cold chicken.

MRS. R. BILLINGS.

CABBAGE SOUP.

Boil a small soup bone, to the stock add a small head of cabbage chopped fine, one teacup of rice, a little chopped celery,(or celery salt) and boil until soft.

MRS. NELSON ALLAIR.

CABBAGE SOUP.

One quart of chopped cabbage, one quart of water, cook one-half hour. Be sure you have the same quantity before adding milk. Add one quart of milk, season with butter, pepper and salt. This quantity will serve three or four persons.

MRS. M. F. SAMPSON.

PEA SOUP.

One quart of split peas soaked over night, next morning let them boil until soft, and then pass them through a fine sieve, after which mix with it stock if you have it, if not add water to make it as thin as you wish and a small piece of butter, pepper and salt.

MRS. A. H. GRAVES.

CLAM SOUP.

Two dozen clams chopped fine, pour over them one quart of cold water and let them just simmer, nothing more, on the back of the stove three-quarters of an hour, then add one pint of milk, season with butter, pepper, salt; soup is improved by adding from one-half to a tablespoon of Worcestershire Sauce.

MRS. A. H. GRAVES.

POTATO SOUP.

One quart of milk, six large potatoes, one stalk of celery, one tablespoon butter, one large onion. Boil in double boiler with celery and onion. Pare and boil potatoes thirty minutes, turn off the water and mash fine; season with salt, pepper and butter; add to the boiling milk; strain and serve immediately. A cup of whipped cream added after the soup is in the tureen improves it.

MRS. R. M. WOODS.

TURKEY SOUP.

Take a carcass of roast chicken or turkey, leaving on some of the dressing. Cover with cold water and boil several hours. Cut into this one stalk of celery, and boil one hour longer.

MRS. R. BILLINGS.

CLAM CHOWDER.

One-half peck clams, wash shells with brush and boil. Fry four slices of salt pork crisp, in frying pan, (cut fine before frying.) Take out pork, and fry brown four onions sliced thin. Take clams from shells and chop fine, strain broth that clams were boiled in, and put back into kettle, add chopped clams, pork, onions, three or four sliced potatoes, salt and pepper to taste; boil slowly one hour Just before serving add spoonful of flour to thicken slightly. Add milk if desired.

MRS. J. E. PORTER.

BEAN SOUP.

One pint of steamed beans; rub through a colander or remove skins, place on stove, and add one pint of milk with salt and a little red pepper. Also one onion sliced and fried in butter. Butter two slices of bread, cut them in dice, brown them in the oven Add to the soup just before serving. Potatoes, peas, asparagus or tomatoes can be used in the same way.

MISS MILLER.

CELERY SOUP.

One quart of milk, one pint of water, one large head of celery, two tablespoons flour, one tablespoon butter, one onion, grating of nutmeg. Boil celery in the water forty minutes. Boil milk, onion and nutmeg together. Mash celery in the water in which it has been boiled; add the flour and butter to the milk; add the mashed celery, strain and serve.

MRS. R. M. WOODS.

BLACK BEAN SOUP.—(FINE.)

One pint black beans, two quarts cold water, one small onion, one lemon, two hard boiled eggs, two teaspoons salt, one tablespoon flour, two tablespoons butter, one saltspoon pepper, one saltspoon mustard, one-quarter saltspoon cayenne. Soak the beans over night, in morning drain and put to boil in the cold water. Slice the onions and fry in butter, and put it with the beans and simmer four or five hours until they are soft, adding water as needed, so there will be about two quarts when done. Then rub the beans through strainer, put soup on to boil again, add salt, pepper and mustard. While boiling add the butter and flour which have been cooked together. Cut the lemon and eggs in thin slices, and put in tureen and pour soup over them.

MISS M. A. MORTON.

HAM AND EGG SOUP.

Re-heat three pints of the liquor in which ham has been boiled, (if not too salt) and when boiling, skim, stir in gradually two tablespoonfuls of flour wet in a cup of the cold liquor. Bring to a boil and pour into tureen in which two well beaten eggs and a tablespoonful of chopped parsley with six round crackers split have been placed.

MRS. C. E. HUBBARD.

ASPARAGUS SOUP.

Boil one quart of finely cut asparagus, tender in one quart of water, rub all through a colander. Heat one pint of milk, warm and rub together one tablespoonful of butter with two of flour, adding the hot milk gradually. Season and pour into asparagus. Bring to a boiling point, pour into tureen with a cup of toasted bits of bread.
MRS. C. E. HUBBARD.

MILK SOUP.

One quart of milk, one tablespoon butter, one teaspoonful chopped onion, one-half tablespoon flour, one stalk celery, one teaspoon salt, one half saltspoon white pepper, speck of cayenne, one-half teaspoonful of celery salt, cook milk, onion, celery twenty minutes in double boiler; cook the flour and butter together five minutes being careful not to burn it, then pour it into the soup, add the seasoning and it is ready to finish in any way, if for *Potato Soup* add three boiled potatoes mashed very fine to the foundation, rub through a sieve into hot tureen, if for *Celery* add one pint stewed and sifted celery to the foundation and strain over one egg beaten to a cream.
MRS. GEO. BILLINGS.

TURNIP AND POTATO SOUP.

One cup mashed potato, one cup of mashed turnip, one sliced onion, one pint water. Simmer together, add one pint of hot milk. Butter, salt and pepper to taste. Strain and serve.
MRS. CHARLES GRAVES.

PARSNIP STEW.

One cup meat stock (lamb preferred,) four cold parsnips cut up into dice, four cold potatoes cut in the same manner, two onions, one quart water, cook about one-half hour, or until onion is cooked. Season to taste and serve.
MISS E. SHATTUCK.

LAMB SOUP.

In buying lamb chops, buy the whole piece from which they are cut; have it cut into chops, using the rest for soup. Wash thoroughly rubbing the outside with a coarse towel. Put on the fire in cold water, and boil until meat drops from the bones. Strain and set away till cold. Remove every bit of fat when you wish to use the soup. Put in your tureen one-half cup of rice, which you have steamed till very tender. When the soup is boiling hot, beat an egg and stir it into a cup of milk in which a tablespoon of flour has been rubbed; put with this, a little at a time some of the scalding liquor, until there is no danger of the egg curdling. Serve instantly as it will thicken by standing; season with pepper and salt.

MRS. J. S. WELLS.

SOUP STOCK.

If you buy fresh meat for a soup stock, the shank is most economical. Wash and put on in cold water and one spoonful of salt. When it comes to a boil, take off the scum, and set the kettle where it will boil slowly ten hours. Then strain into a bright tin, or stone pot. In the morning skim off all the fat, turn the jelly out, and take off all the sediment. Use the meat for hash. Do not boil vegetables with this stock as it causes it to sour quickly.

Use celery in all kinds of soup when you can obtain it.

FISH.

"There's as good a fish in the sea as ever was caught."

BAKED FISH.—A LA CREME.

Boil four pounds halibut, when done skin and remove bones, and flake it. Boil one quart of milk, with one half onion chopped fine, a few sprigs of parsley, cayenne pepper and salt. Thicken the milk with three tablespoons flour or butter size of an egg. Butter a dish, put in a layer of fish and then cream, then fish, until it is all used, having cream on top. Sprinkle with sifted bread or cracker crumbs, and bake one-half hour. Garnish with parsley and slices of hard boiled egg.

MRS. G. W. C., N. Y.

HOLLANDAISE SAUCE FOR FISH.

Half tea cup of butter, juice of one-half a lemon, yolks of two eggs, a speck of cayenne, one-half cup boiling water, one-half teaspoon of salt. Beat butter to a cream, add yolks of eggs one by one, then lemon juice, pepper and salt. Place the bowl containing the mixture in a saucepan of boiling water; beat with an egg beater until it begins to thicken, which will be in about a minute, then add boiling water, beating all the time. As soon as it is like soft custard, it is done. For fish and meats, to be poured around the article on the dish.

MISS PARLOA.

BROILED OYSTERS.

Salt and pepper large oysters, dip in melted butter, then in cracker crumbs. Broil over hot coals until brown.

MRS. CUTLER.

OYSTER FRITTERS.

One cup milk, three eggs, one dozen rolled crackers, one tablespoon flour. Place a large oyster in a tablespoon of batter and fry in hot lard.

MRS. R. BILLINGS.

TO FRY OYSTERS.

Dry a few moments in a cloth, dip each one in beaten egg, and then into sifted cracker crumbs. Fry in just enough fat to brown them, put pepper and salt on before turning them over.

RHODE ISLAND FISH CAKES.

One cup of salt cod fish and two cups potatoes cut in small pieces, boil together until tender, then mash together, beat one egg, a little butter, three tablespoons of cream, and add to the fish and potato, beat well, drop with a spoon into hot fat. Bacon fat is the best if you have it.

MRS. EDWARD ELDRIDGE.

ESCALLOPED FISH.

One pound of fresh boiled cod fish, then make a sauce of one tablespoon of butter, two of flour stirred into one pint of boiling milk until it thickens, cut hard boiled egg into sauce then pour all into a deep dish first a layer of fish then a layer of sauce until dish is filled, cover top with cracker crumbs and bake one-half hour.

MRS. H. L. WILLIAMS.

FRIED SALT COD FISH.

Soak salt cod fish twenty-four hours, changing the water three times, drain thoroughly, roll in egg batter and fry.

M. A. MORTON.

ESCALLOPED OYSTERS.

Three pints of oysters, fifteen rolled crackers, one pint of milk, three eggs, butter, salt and pepper.

MRS. CHAS. JONES.

BAKED FISH.

Make a dressing of bread crumbs. Stuff the fish and sew or tie securely. Place in a pan with some hot water, lay pieces of pork on top with a little pepper and salt and bake, basting very often.

MRS. F. H. BARDWELL.

ESCALLOPED SALMON.

Prepare with rolled cracker; butter, pepper and salt in layer, same as for oysters. Pour milk over them, and last of all beat one egg, and spread over the top and bake.

MRS. DOUGHERTY.

ESCALLOPED OYSTERS.

Take bread crumbs, rolled fine; put layer in bottom of dish; season with butter, salt and pepper, then layer of oysters and so on until dish is nearly full. Cover tightly and bake twenty minutes or half an hour, then remove cover and bake until done. Use no wetting.

MRS. J. E. PORTER.

FISH CROQUETTES.

One pint each of finely minced cold boiled fish and mashed potato, wet with one-half cup hot milk, one egg and salt and pepper, mix well, shape, dip in egg then in crumbs and fry brown.

MEATS.

*The body craveth meats, the spirit athirst for peacefulness,
He that hath these, hath enough.* (Tupper.)

ROAST TURKEY, CHICKEN OR DUCK.

Wash the fowl and wipe dry, and stuff the breast and body with the following dressing For a fowl weighing between seven and eight pounds, take one quart of stale bread and crumb very fine; add a tablespoon of salt, a scant teaspoon of pepper, a teaspoon of chopped parsley, one teaspoon powdered sage, one of summer savory, a half cup of butter and a little milk. Mix well together. Sew up the fowl, tie legs and wings close to the body, rub well with butter, pepper, salt and flour. Sew up in a cloth and baste often, turn the fowl over when about half done.

ROAST VEAL.

Cut gashes all over the meat, and fill them with dressing, and sprinkle salt, pepper and flour over the surface; baste frequently.

SPICED VEAL.

Boil three or four pounds of veal until tender, then chop it fine and season with salt and pepper, and very little sage and very little clover; return to the liquor you boiled the veal in, leaving only enough to moisten your chopped meat, then pour this into a square tin, set in a cool place to harden.

VEAL CUTLETS.

One pound veal steak, remove all fat and bones, shape nicely into round flat pieces about the size of doughnuts, pound out, skewer into good shape, sprinkle with salt and pepper, roll in sifted bread crumbs, then egg, then crumbs last, fry in pork fat fifteen minutes, a handsome brown, all over the same, lay them in a stew pan, carefully make the following sauce: One tablespoonful butter, one tablespoonful flour, mix smoothly, add a cupfull hot water or stock made from the trimmings of the veal; pinch of pepper, one tablespoon lemon juice, or vinegar or mixed horse-radish; cook the cutlets, just simmer them three-fourths of an hour.

TO WARM-OVER MEAT.

Butter a dish; put in a layer of mashed seasoned potatoes, then any kind of meat you wish to utilize, chopped fine; season with salt, pepper and butter to taste; then more mashed potatoes, and so on until the dish is full; the top layer should be potatoes, bake one-half hour; serve hot.

SCALLOPED CHICKEN.

One pound chicken meat, cut in small bits as for salad; one cup fine dry bread crumbs, one coffee cup of chicken broth or jelly, three cups rich milk, two tablespoons butter, two eggs, two tablespoons corn starch, salt and pepper. Put the milk in a sauce pan and when boiling hot add the corn starch wet with a little milk, add butter, crumbs and broth; season all to taste. Butter a baking dish, line with a thick layer of bread crumbs, pour in the mixture, put a layer of crumbs on top and a few bits of butter. Bake three quarters of an hour.

MRS. A. F. CURTIS.

ROAST PORK.

Wipe and dredge with flour, salt, pepper and sage. Place in hot oven for two hours then baste frequently, and bake one hour.

ROAST LAMB.

Take a leg of lamb weighing six pounds, wipe with a damp cloth, steam two hours, then sprinkle with salt, flour and pepper. Bake one hour, while baking baste often.

LAMB STEWED WITH PEAS.

Cut breast of lamb in pieces, place in a pan, cover and let it simmer for twenty minutes. Skim, and add a tablespoon of salt and one quart of shelled peas, cover, and stew for half an hour. Mix a tablespoon of flour and two of butter and stir into the stew. Simmer fifteen minutes longer and serve.

FRIZZLED BEEF.

Shave dried beef, put in a frying pan. Add milk and a piece of butter, thicken with flour, add one egg just before removing from the fire.

MRS. R. BILLINGS.

BROILED BEEFSTEAK.

A steak cut about three-quarters of an inch thick, well pounded. Place immediately over hot coals, on a hot gridiron. Thoroughly brown on one side before turning. When done sprinkle with salt and pepper; place on a hot platter and spread with softened butter. Send at once to the table.

MRS. A. F. CURTIS.

GRILLED CHICKEN.

Take a young and tender chicken and halve it. Rub well with butter and flour; sprinkle with salt and pepper. Lay in a well buttered dripping-pan, place in a hot oven and bake about an hour. Serve with giblet sauce.

MRS. A. H. GRAVES.

MUTTON PIE PLAIN.

Take cold mutton cut in thin slices; put in pudding dish and season with salt and pepper; mix two tablespoons of flour with cold water, then pour on to this one pint of boiling water; season and pour over the meat. Make a paste as for plain pie crust, and cover it. Bake one hour.

CHICKEN PIE.

Boil three chickens until tender; place a layer of chicken in pan, add butter, pepper and salt; then another layer of chicken and so on until the pan is filled, pour in broth of chicken. Cover with a baking powder crust made as follows: Three pints of flour, four teaspoons baking powder, three tablespoons shortening, three cups of milk, salt. Place a little butter on top of pie before baking.

POT ROAST.

Take a good sized piece of meat for boiling. Sear over all sides by placing in a hot kettle and turning until all the sides are brown. Place water enough in the kettle to keep from burning, and cover closely to keep in steam. Cook slowly four or five hours (adding water as it boils away.) At the last allow nearly all the water to boil away and make a brown gravy if desired by adding a little flour and butter and boiling water.

MRS. R. BILLINGS.

MOCK DUCK.

Spread a round steak with butter or pork fat, salt, pepper, and dredge with flour, prepare a dressing of one cup bread crumbs (soaked,) one egg, one-half chopped onion, a little chopped pork, salt and pepper, spread the dressing on the steak and roll as you would roll jelly cake, tie in place, basting frequently, serve with a gravy, cut into rounds.

MRS. CHARLES GRAVES.

ESCALLOPED MEAT.

Take cold roast beef or chicken, chop fine, butter a deep dish and fill with alternate layers of bread crumbs and meat, season with salt, pepper and butter, moisten with milk or beef gravy. Bake one-half hour.

MRS. F. H. BARDWELL.

ESCALLOPED MEAT.

Boil pieces of roast beef until tender, when cold strain out all fat and take meat out of the stock, chop meat fine, salt and pepper. Cook one quart of canned tomatoes with an onion sliced in it for half an hour, strain this, add the tomato juice to the seasoned meat, a pint of bread or cracker crumbs, butter a baking dish put in a layer of crumbs well moistened with stock, on this put a layer of seasoned meat, another layer of crumbs and stock and meat, dot the top with bits of butter, bake in a moderate oven three-quarters of an hour.

MRS. R. M. WOODS.

STUFFED BEEF.

Take a beefsteak, (round) pound well. Make a good dressing, (same as for turkey) and roll inside, pin together with skewers, dust with flour. Season well and bake quickly, about three quarters of an hour. Have the pan hot.

MRS. A. H. GRAVES.

BEEF A LA MODE.

The day before using, take about six pounds of round of beef, gash it at intervals to receive strips of salt pork, half an inch wide. Have several tablespoons full of chopped carrots and onion, also whole spices, pepper corns, allspice, cloves, salt and press some into the meat, and lay the remainder over it for the night. In the morning put all into a large pot, and nearly cover with hot water, close pot and boil until tender, boiling water away, and browning in pot. Take out meat, and add water enough to make gravy in the same pot, and pour over meat on platter. Must cook many hours. Excellent to re-heat another day.

MISS NETTIE MORTON.

POTTED HAM.

Cut all the meat, fat and lean, from a boiled ham, chop very fine and pound to a paste, to each pint of paste add one teaspoonful mustard, a speck of cayenne pepper, a little garlic, and if not fat enough a tablespoon of butter, pack in a small earthen jar, paste paper over the top and put on the cover, place the jar in a baking pan of hot water in the oven, bake slowly two hours, when cold take of cover and pour over melted butter. Cover again and set away in cool place.

MRS. M. E. MILLER.

PRESSED CHICKEN.

Boil a chicken until tender, take the meat from the bones, season with salt, pepper and butter, pour in enough of the liquor it was boiled in to moisten well and pour in any shape you choose, placing alternate layers of light and dark meat, when cold turn out and slice.

MRS. R. BILLINGS.

VEAL PATTIE.

Three pounds of veal chopped fine, one pound of salt pork, one coffeecup of rolled crackers, two teaspoons salt, two small teaspoons of pepper, four eggs, mix thoroughly, and bake two hours in a slow oven.

MRS. KNIGHT.

ROUND STEAK.

Chop round steak thoroughly on both sides, but leave it in one piece, season with salt, pepper, and place in a hot spider in which you have before placed a piece of butter, fry brown.

FRIED TRIPE.

Take good fat honeycomb tripe, let stand in hot water a few moments, drain, and wipe dry, dip in egg, and then roll in fine cracker crumbs, fry in butter or fat until a delicate brown on both sides, lay on platter, and add a little butter and salt. Serve hot.

MUTTON PIE WITH TOMATOES.

Chop mutton fine as for hash, put in dish and season with salt, pepper, and butter, then a layer of sliced tomatoes, then soft boiled rice spread on top, a little more butter, bake three-quarters of an hour.

MEAT PIE.

Pieces of cold roast beef may be placed in a baking dish and seasoned with salt, pepper, butter and a little wetting. A baking powder crust may be placed over this, or some prefer mashed potato.

RAGOUT OF MEAT.

Two cups chopped cold meat, one cup rolled cracker, season with salt and pepper, moisten with milk or beef gravy, shape into balls, roll in cracker crumbs, then in egg, again in crumbs, bake in a hot oven fifteen minutes or until brown.

MRS. CUTLER.

BEEFSTEAK SMOTHERED IN ONIONS.

Fry brown four slices of salt pork, when brown take out the pork and put in six onions sliced thin, fry ten minutes stirring all the time, then take out all except a thin layer, and upon this lay a slice of steak, then a layer of onions, then steak and cover with onions, dredge each layer with salt, pepper and flour, pour over this one cupful of boiling water, and cover tight, simmer half an hour. When you dish place the steak in center of dish and heap the onions around it.

BEEFSTEAK OMELET.

One and one-half pounds steak, chop fine, add one egg, small piece of butter, little salt, half cup milk, bake half an hour.

MRS. CHARLES BARTLETT.

VEAL LOAF.—EXCELLENT.

Four pounds lean veal, well done, and one pound raw salt pork, chop together fine, add one tablespoon pepper, salt, two tablespoons of sage, four tablespoons of bread crumbs, four eggs and half pint sweet cream, mix eggs, cream, bread crumbs and seasoning together, then add the meat and mix thoroughly, press into a deep dish and bake four hours, lay bits of butter on top before baking, to be eaten cold, slice thin.

BEEF LOAF.

Three pounds fresh beef chopped fine, two cups cracker crumbs, one and one-half cups sweet milk, two eggs, butter the size of an egg, salt, pepper and sage if you choose, bake slowly two hours.

MRS. C. L. WARNER.

GRAVIES AND SAUCES FOR MEATS.

GIBLET SAUCE.

Take heart, livers and gizzard; (chicken) boil, chop fine; make a drawn butter gravy; add the giblets; season with salt and pepper.

BROWN GRAVY SAUCE.

Set the pan in which the meat was roasted on the range; add boiling water, scrape toward the center the browned flour from the sides and bottom, thicken with small quantity of flour, season with butter, pepper and salt, to be used with roast beef.

OYSTER SAUCE.

Make drawn butter gravy, season to taste, add raw oysters, chopped a little. Nice to eat with roast turkey.

MINT SAUCE.

To two tablespoons of chopped mint, add one tablespoon of white sugar, and nearly two-thirds of a cup of vinegar. Let them stand ten minutes in a cool place before sending to table.

MARION HARLAND.

CAPER SAUCE FOR LEG OF LAMB.

Make drawn butter gravy from drippings left from steaming, add capers more or less, season with pepper and salt.

GRAVY FOR BOILED OR BAKED FISH.

One-quarter pound butter, large spoon flour, thoroughly mixed. One cup boiling water. Salt if needed. Take the yolks of two hard boiled eggs, pulverize and add to the above. Cook three minutes before egg is added.

BREAD SAUCE.

Two cups of milk, one cup of bread crumbs, one-quarter of a good sized onion; one tablespoon of butter, salt and pepper to taste, let onion and milk come to a boil together, have bread very dry, roll fine and sift through a flour sieve put in milk and cook ten minutes, then take out the onion and add butter and seasoning. Put tablespoon of butter in a small fry pan, when very hot add coarse crumbs and stir constantly until crisp and brown, sprinkle over birds or game of any kind and pour sauce around and serve.

TOMATO SAUCE.

One quart can tomatoes, two tablespoons of butter, two of flour, two cloves and a small slice of onion. Cook tomatoes onions and cloves ten minutes, heat the butter in frying pan and add the flour, stir into the tomato and cook ten minutes, season to taste with salt and pepper and put through a strainer. Nice for fish and meat.

TARTARE SAUCE.

Yolks of two uncooked eggs, one-half cup olive oil, three tablespoons vinegar, one tablespoon mustard, one teaspoon sugar, one-quarter teaspoon pepper, one teaspoon salt, one teaspoon onion juice, one tablespoon of chopped capers, one tablespoon chopped cucumber pickles. Beat yolks well and add seasoning and mustard mixed together add drop by drop the oil alternately with the vinegar beating all the while, then add capers and cucumber pickles. Serve with fish or cauliflower.

M. K. BARNES.

VEGETABLES.

Cheerful looks make every dish a feast. (Massinger.)

VEGETABLES—PREPARING AND COOKING.

All green vegetables must be washed in cold water and dropped into water which has been salted and just beginning to boil. There should be a tablespoon of salt to every two quarts of water. The younger and more freshly gathered the more quickly they are cooked.

Potatoes, boiled,	Thirty to forty minutes.
Potatoes, baked,	Forty-five minutes.
Sweet Potatoes, boiled,	Forty-five minutes.
Squash, boiled,	Twenty-five minutes.
Squash, baked,	Forty-five minutes.
Green Peas, boiled,	Twenty to forty minutes.
Shell Beans,	One hour.
String Beans,	One to two hours.
Green Corn,	Twenty-five minutes.
Asparagus,	Fifteen to thirty minutes.
Spinach,	One to two hours.
Cabbage,	Forty-five minutes to two hours.
Dandelion Greens,	Two to three hours.
Beet Greens,	One hour.
Onions,	One to two hours.
Beets,	One to five hours.
White Turnips,	Forty-five minutes.
Parsnips,	Thirty to forty minutes.
Carrots,	One to two hours.

POTATO SOUFFLE.

Boil four good sized potatoes, pass them through a sieve, scald one-half cup milk and one tablespoon butter add to the potato with a little salt and pepper, and beat to a cream, add (one at a time) the yolks of four eggs, beating thoroughly, drop into the whites a small pinch of salt, and beat to a stiff froth add to mixture, beating as little as possible. Bake twenty minutes in well buttered baking dish. Serve at once, to be eaten with meats that have gravies.

STUFFED AND BAKED TOMATOES.

Take as many tomatoes as your dish will hold, smooth, and solid Cut a small piece from top, and carefully remove the pulp and seeds. Make a dressing of bread crumbs, seasoned with pepper, salt and sage, mix with pulp carefully, stuff tomatoes and add a piece of butter on the top of each. Bake about half an hour.

TO BOIL CAULIFLOWER.

Put into boiling water, and boil briskly from twenty minutes to one-half hour keeping the sauce pan uncovered, skimming the water several times. When tender, drain and place in the dish. Serve with butter, a white sauce or drawn butter.

STUFFED POTATOES.

Take large, fair potatoes, bake until soft, cut small piece from one end, and carefully remove the inside without breaking the skin. Prepare as for mashed potato using milk, butter, salt and pepper to taste. Stuff the potatoes and put in oven to keep hot until wanted for table.

MRS. G. W. C.

BOILED DINNER.

Wash a piece of corned beef weighing about five pounds, put into one gallon of cold water, when it comes to a boil, skim carefully and boil slowly three hours. At the beginning of the last two hours add a large head of cabbage, cut in two. An hour later add carrots and turnips nicely cleaned. Lastly add potatoes, allowing one-half hour for them to boil. Cook beets in a separate kettle.

MRS. C. E. HUBBARD.

BOILING VEGETABLES.

In boiling beef and vegetables, put a tea cup of vinegar into the pot when the water is cold, and the beef will be much tenderer, and cabbage and beets better flavored and will not fill the house with unpleasant smell. The vinegar will not affect the taste of food. RULE:—All vegetables to go into fast boiling water, to be quickly brought to the boiling point again, not left to steep in the hot water before boiling, which toughens them and destroys color and flavor.

MRS. CHARLES E. HUBBARD.

POTATO BALLS.

Take four large mealy cold potatoes and mash in a pan with two tablespoons of melted butter, a pinch of salt and a little pepper, one tablespoon of cream and the beaten yolk of one egg. Rub all together for about five minutes or until very soft, shape into round balls dip them into fine sifted bread crumbs and fry in boiling lard.

S. G. LANGDON.

FRIED PARSNIPS.

Boil until tender remove the skin and cool, cut in lengthwise nice slices, and fry in hot lard or pork fat, until nicely browned, season with pepper, salt, and butter, serve hot.

A NICE WAY TO COOK CABBAGE.

With a sharp knife cut a small cabbage into small pieces, boil one hour in salted water, drain through a colander, take one cup sweet milk, piece of butter size of an egg, a little salt, heat hot, but do not boil, put the cabbage into this mixture and let stand on stove until well warmed through. Dish, sprinkle with pepper, send to the table hot and although cabbage it is really delicate. Onions, cooked the same way are equally nice.

MRS. A. F. CURTIS.

STEWED CABBAGE.

Cut a head of cabbage fine as for slaw, and boil half an hour in clear water, pour off this water and cover with salted water, and cook until tender, drain, pour over this a dressing made of one-half cup of cream, one-half cup sweet milk, and one tablespoon of flour, stirred together until smooth; this is good either hot or cold and will not hurt the most delicate stomach.

MRS. F. CARL.

TREMONT POTATOES.

Take cold boiled potatoes of uniform medium size, and split lengthwise into quarters or sixths, fry like doughnuts in boiling lard until the outside is browned or crisped. Skim out and drain, sprinkle a little salt on them before serving.

BAKED RICE AND TOMATOES.

One pint of rice, boil from twelve to fifteen minutes; pour off water through a colander, put the rice into a steamer for one hour or until dry, and each grain is like pop corn. Have your tomatoes boiled and pour over rice. Butter and salt and pepper to taste. Bake until brown, and serve hot.

BEET HASH.

Add usual quantity of meat and potato, one-third quantity of boiled beets moisten with cream if possible, if not use milk, can be made with or without meat, season to taste.
MRS. A. L. BARDWELL.

PARSNIP FRITTERS.

Mash parsnips fine, then add one tablespoonful flour, one egg, season, butter, salt, pepper, make patties, and fry in butter.
MISS E. SHATTUCK.

MACARONI BOILED.

Break up and wash a pint bowl full of macaroni, put in a shallow basin and cover with cold water, set this basin into another, and place on the fire, after fifteen minutes add a pint of milk and a teaspoon of salt. Let it cook ten minutes longer, then add a spoonful of butter and cook five minutes longer. The macaroni left from one dinner can be used by placing in a buttered shallow dish, then grate cheese over it and brown.
MISS PARLOA.

MACARONI IN CREAM.

Wash a pint of macaroni, and put in a basin with cold milk, set this in another basin with some water and let it stand twenty minutes on the fire, then take off and when it gets cold stir in one teaspoon of salt, and three well beaten eggs, turn into shallow dish and bake twenty minutes.

AN OLD-FASHIONED DISH.

Fry several slices of salt pork brown, and take from the spider, place in the fat, sliced sour apples cover and fry, take these out and put in potatoes sliced thin, serve apples and potatoes with pork.

BAKED BEANS.

Soak one quart of beans over night pour off the water, and cook in fresh water until they crack open, then put them in an earthen dish, cover with water. (Add a little molasses if you like them sweet) Put in center of the dish one half pound of salt pork, parboiled, and scored across the rind. Bake slowly four hours, until brown

BREAKFAST AND TEA DISHES.

"Dinner may be pleasant.
So may social tea;
But yet methinks the breakfast
Is best of all the three."

DUCHESS POTATOES.

Boil potatoes as usual to mash, when done, drain, and add two ounces of butter, two eggs, a bit of white pepper and salt. Press through a sieve, form into little oval loaves, flat on top, mark with a knife, put melted butter on top, and brown in oven.

MISS. LUCY WEBBER.

ESCOLLOPED POTATOES.

Butter a deep dish and fill with cold sliced potatoes, sprinkle salt over the potatoes, scald one quart of milk, boil two tablespoons butter on stove, when boiling add one-half cup of flour, then stir in gradually the milk, until it thickens, seasoning with salt and pepper. Then pour in the potatoes, place cracker crumbs on top mixed with melted butter. Bake one-half hour.

MRS. F. H. BARDWELL.

POTATO CAKES.

Two cups mashed potatoes, one beaten egg, one tablespoon melted butter, salt and pepper. Form into balls, roll in flour and fry in hot lard.

MRS. C. A. JONES.

RISOTTO NAPOLITAINE.

One onion, one ounce butter, one pound rice, one quart beef stock, three ounces grated cheese. Cut a medium sized onion into small pieces, and put into sauce pan on stove with one ounce of butter. Cook about fifteen minutes or until lightly colored. Wash the rice, blanch ten minutes in boiling water, then put in cold water for a minute, drain and put in sauce pan with onion and beef stock. Simmer gently for fifty minutes and add the grated cheese, dash of pepper, salt and cayenne. Stir well together boil a few minutes, and serve hot.

MISS M. K. BARNES.

GRAHAM GRIDDLE CAKES.

Two quarts of sweet milk or skim milk, two tablespoons of molasses, five teaspoons of salt, one-half of a yeast cake, one quart and half of graham flour, one quart and a fourth of wheat flour. Stir all together the night before. Let rise until morning, then fry on a hot iron, and serve immediately. Cakes for a family of nine.

MRS. F. H. BARDWELL.

POTATO CROQUETTES.

Six large cooked potatoes, one tablespoon of butter; one wineglass of cream, yolks of two eggs, salt to taste. Peel, boil and mash potatoes until perfectly smooth, then add the butter, cream and lastly eggs. Shape as croquettes, dip in egg and bread and cracker crumbs, and fry in boiling lard a nice brown. It would be well after mixing to let stand in a cold place for an hour.

MISS HARRIET BYRNE.

SWEET BREADS ON TOAST.

Boil sweet breads twenty minutes, remove the skin, and tough fibre. Make cream sauce of one pint milk thickened with tablespoon of flour when boiling, and a little butter and salt. Cut the sweet breads into dice and add to the boiling sauce, boil a minute and serve on pieces of toast.

MISS M. K. BARNES.

CROQUETTES.

One cup chopped lobster or chicken, one saltspoon of dry mustard, one saltspoon of salt, a little pepper. Make white sauce as follows: One cup scalded milk, two tablespoons butter, two tablespoons flour. Stir butter and flour 'till smooth. Add hot milk and chopped meat. When cool roll a large spoon of the mixture in cracker or bread crumbs, then in beaten egg, then in crumbs again. Fry in hot fat until brown.

MRS. I. B. LOWELL.

RICE OMELET.

One cup cold boiled rice, four teaspoons milk, two eggs, whites and yolks beaten separately, one-half saltspoon salt, one tablespoon butter. Heat butter very hot in frying pan, then pour in other ingredients mixed well together. Cover and bake about ten minutes in moderate oven, until stiff. Double and turn it out carefully onto hot platter.

MRS. A. H. GRAVES.

VEAL PATTEE.

Three pounds finely chopped veal, one pound salt pork, one coffee cup rolled crackers, two tea spoons salt, two small tea spoons pepper, four eggs, mix thoroughly, bake two hours in slow oven.

MRS. KNIGHT.

RICE CROQUETTES.

One large cup cooked rice, one-half cup milk, one egg, one tablespoon of sugar, one tablespoon butter, one-half teaspoon salt, little grating of nutmeg. Put milk in a dish and add rice and seasoning. When it boils up, add the well beaten egg. Stir a minute, then take off and cool. When cold, shape and roll well in egg and crumbs, drop in boiling lard and fry until brown.
MISS M. K. BARNES.

CHICKEN CROQUETTES.

Two finely chopped cups chicken, butter size of an egg, one large spoon flour, one large cup of water, one-half teacup of milk. Melt butter and flour together, then add milk and water. Cook this to consistency of drawn butter. Then add cup bread crumbs. Season with salt and pepper, then add chicken and cook slowly a few moments. When done spread in a dish to cool, then make into balls, dip in beaten egg, roll in cracker crumbs and fry in boiling lard. This rule makes twelve. Veal can be used instead of chicken.
MRS. A. H. GRAVES.

CHICKEN CROQUETTES.

One solid pint of finely chopped chicken or lamb, (cooked,) one tablespoon salt, one-half teaspoon pepper one cup cream or chicken stock, one tablespoon flour, four eggs, one teaspoon onion juice, one tablespoon lemon juice, one pint bread crumbs, little parsley, three tablespoons butter. Put stock or cream on to boil. Mix flour and butter together and stir into it. Then add chicken and seasoning. Boil for two minutes and add two of the eggs, well beaten. Then take from fire and set away to cool. When cold, shape and fry, using the other two eggs to dip the balls into.
MRS. G. B. BARNES.

CHICKEN SOUFFLE.

One pint finely chopped cooked chicken, one pint cream sauce, four eggs, one tablespoon onion juice, salt and pepper. Stir the chicken into the boiling sauce, cook two minutes. Add the yolks of the eggs well beaten, and set away to cool. Then add the whites well beaten. Turn into a buttered dish and bake half an hour.

MRS. G. B. BARNES.

ESCOLLOPED POTATOES.

Butter the bottom and sides of a tin basin, slice cold boiled potatoes, place in the basin a layer of potatoes, butter, pepper and salt, dust flour over it. Another layer of potatoes, with seasoning and so on, until the dish is filled. Place on top a layer of cracker crumbs, and over the whole a large cup of cream. Bake in steady oven half an hour.

CREAM POTATOES.

One pint cold chopped potatoes, one cup milk, one tablespoon flour, one teaspoon salt. Heat milk in a sauce pan, stir flour in cold milk until smooth, add to the boiling milk, put potatoes into the cream and stir until well heated, add tablespoon of butter and put into oven to brown.

MRS. B. M. WARNER.

SMOTHERED SAUSAGE.

Prick link sausages with large needle in fifteen or twenty places. Put in frying pan in which is half cup hot water, roll sausages over in this several times and cover closely. Put the pan where the water will boil slowly for ten minutes, roll sausages over again two or three times and cook the other side ten minutes. Turn twice more, at intervals of five minutes. Cover and let steam five minutes before serving.

MRS. D. BILLINGS.

PRESSED CHICKEN.

Boil a chicken until tender, take the meat from the bones, season with salt, pepper and butter. Pour in enough of the liquor it was boiled in to moisten well, and put in any shape you choose, placing alternate layers of light and dark meat. When cold turn out and slice.

MRS. R. BILLINGS.

BEEF LOAF.

Three pounds fresh beef chopped fine, two cups cracker crumbs, one and one-half cups sweet milk, two eggs, butter size of an egg, salt, pepper and sage if you choose. Bake slowly two hours.

MRS. C. L. WARNER.

VEAL LOAF.

Two pounds uncooked veal, chopped very fine, one-half pound salt pork, chopped very fine, two eggs, one pound pounded crackers, three tablespoons of salt, two tablespoons of pepper, one tablespoon of sugar, little sage. Press hard and bake two hours.

MRS. PEASE.

APPLE FRITTERS.

Two eggs, one cup of milk, one cup flour, one teaspoon of baking powder, three apples sliced thin, little salt. Drop in hot fat, a tablespoon at a time. Brown like doughnuts, sprinkle on sugar while hot.

MRS. I. B. LOWELL.

SNOWY OMELET.

Four eggs, four tablespoons of milk, little salt and pepper, beat yolks separately, mix together, leaving out one-third of the whites, when ready to turn spread one-half the remaining whites. In making omelet, when it has set round the edge, set in the oven four minutes, then take out and turn.

MRS. S. G. HUBBARD.

BEEF STEAK OMELET.

One and one-half pound steak, chop fine, one egg, small piece butter, little salt, one-half cup milk. Bake one-half an hour.

MRS. CHARLES BARTLETTE.

MEAT OMELET.

Piece of cold roast beef or steak, chopped fine, to one cup meat add one egg, beaten, salt and pepper. Mix thoroughly, drop a tablespoon on a hot buttered griddle brown both sides. Chopped oysters may be used.

MRS. CUTLER.

RAGOUT OF MEAT.

Two cups chopped cold meat, one cup rolled cracker, season with salt and pepper, moisten with milk or beef gravy, shape into balls, roll in cracker crumbs, then in eggs, again in crumbs. Bake in hot oven fifteen minutes, or until brown.

MRS. CUTLER.

OMELET.

Four eggs, whites and yolks beaten separately, three tablespoons milk to each egg, one tablespoon of flour, salt, add beaten whites last. Put in spider butter half size of an egg, cover and cook slowly.

MRS. J. E. PORTER.

PRESSED EGGS.

Eight eggs boiled hard, while hot, chop with salt and butter size of a walnut. Press in deep dish and serve cold.

MRS. A. H. GRAVES.

EGG OMELET.

One cup milk, one cup cracker crumbs, three eggs beaten, and a little salt.

MRS. C. W. MARSH.

WELSH RARE BIT.

One-half pound grated cheese, two eggs, one-half cup of cream or milk, one teaspoon mustard, one teaspoon salt, one teaspoon melted butter, speck of cayenne, speck of soda. Melt cheese, when nearly melted add other ingredients and cook until thickened. Serve on split crackers.

MISS EUNICE MORTON.

CORN FRITTERS.

One pint of corn pulp, two beaten eggs, one-half teaspoon of salt, a little pepper, two tablespoons of flour or just enough to keep corn and eggs together.

MRS. C. W. MARSH.

CORN OYSTERS.

One pint of grated sweet corn, one egg well beaten, one small cup of flour, one-half gill of cream, one teaspoon of salt. Fry in hot fat by teaspoonfuls.

MRS. HENRY S. HUBBARD.

HAM AND EGG ON TOAST.

Chop fine pieces of cold boiled ham, toast and butter slices of bread, spread the ham on bread and place in oven about three minutes. Beat six eggs, (less will do) with half cup milk, little pepper and salt. Put in sauce pan with two tablespoons of butter and stir over fire until it begins to thicken, take off and beat for a minute, then spread on toast and ham.

MRS. C. K. MORTON.

BAKED OMELET.

Four eggs, whites, yolks beaten separately, add to yolks one tablespoon flour, two tablespoons melted butter, one cup milk, salt and pepper to taste, stir in whites of eggs. Butter the dish and bake fifteen minutes.

MISS CORNELIA BILLINGS.

BAKED EGGS.

Beat the whites of six eggs to a stiff froth add little salt, place on buttered dish make six holes dropping into each one whole yolk. Bake quickly until whites are slightly brown.

MRS. CUTLER.

WAFFLES.

One pint sweet milk, two heaping teaspoons baking powder, flour to make as thick as griddle cakes. Then add three eggs well beaten, butter size of an egg melted. Fry brown in waffle iron.

WAFFLES.

Three eggs, yolks only, one quart milk, one-half cup melted butter, one heaping teaspoon baking powder. Afterwards add whites of eggs, and flour enough to make stiff batter.

SALADS.

"Now good digestion wait on appetite and health on both."
(Shakespeare.)

CHICKEN OR VEAL SALAD.

Half as much celery as meat, yolks of two eggs, cup of vinegar, one teaspoon strong mustard, piece of butter, salt, teaspoon sugar. Boil all together on stove. Pour over.

CARRIE L. WARNER.

SALAD DRESSING.

Yolks of three eggs, one teaspoon mustard, two teaspoons salt, one-quarter teaspoon cayenne pepper, two tablespoons sugar, one cup cream or milk, one-half cup hot vinegar, whites of three eggs beaten stiff.

MRS. GEO. BILLINGS.

SALAD DRESSING.

Two and a half teaspoons mustard, one cup vinegar, three eggs, little pepper and salt. Boiled together with a cup of butter or cream. When cold add one-third cup of sugar. Just before serving whip a half cup cream and stir into dressing.

MRS. A. H. GRAVES.

ANOTHER.

One egg thoroughly beaten, one teaspoon mustard, one tablespoon sugar, butter size of a walnut, one-half cup vinegar. Mix thoroughly and cook a little.

CABBAGE SALAD.

Shred cabbage fine, sprinkle with salt and pepper, one-half cup vinegar, two tablespoons water, one tablespoon butter, two tablespoons sugar. Let it come to a boil; when cool beat in one-half cup of cream, one egg, one-half tablespoon flour. Let all boil up once, add the cabbage, mix while hot.
S. G. LANGDON.

CREAM SALAD.

Chop fine one-half head of cabbage. Stir into it one-half cup cream and a little salt. Heat one-half cup vinegar stirring into it the beaten yolks of two eggs, one teaspoon sugar, one-half teaspoon mustard. Pour over the cabbage as it goes to the table.
MISS CARRIE WARNER.

CABBAGE SALAD.

One small head of cabbage sliced or chopped fine, one cup sweet milk boiling hot, a little less than a cup of vinegar, one tablespoon butter, two eggs, well beaten, one tablespoon sugar, one teaspoon extract of celery, pepper and salt to taste. Heat milk and vinegar separately, when vinegar boils add the butter, sugar, pepper and salt. Boil up once and stir in the cabbage. Heat to scalding heat (do not boil.) To the hot milk add the eggs and cook one minute after it begins to thicken. Put cabbage into a deep dish, pour on the custard, stirring quickly, tossing up mixture with a silver fork. Cover close and put on ice.
MRS. E. GRAVES.

BOILED DRESSING.

Yolks of three eggs, one teaspoon mustard, one teaspoon salt, a little cayenne, one tablespoon of sugar, two tablespoons melted butter, one-half cup vinegar, one cup cream or milk, mix together and cook like boiled custard. The whites of eggs may be beaten and added just before serving to make more in quantity, but better without.

MRS. M. K. MORTON, MRS. M. H. BURKE.

SALAD DRESSING.

Two eggs beaten light, one-half cup vinegar, one teaspoon each of mustard, sugar and salt, mixed together with a little hot water until smooth. Pour the egg into the mixture, add one cup of cream or butter, and cook in a double boiler until it thickens.

MRS. R. M. WOODS.

LOBSTER SALAD.

Two boiled lobsters chopped with lettuce, not very fine, also the whites of four hard boiled eggs, rub the yolks in a bowl with one teaspoon mustard, one-half teaspoon salt, small teaspoon sugar, little cayenne pepper, butter size of an egg (melted) Add vinegar to taste, a half cup or so. Serve on lettuce leaves after mixing with the dressing.

MRS. E. C. BYRNE.

SALAD DRESSING.

Two well beaten eggs, one tablespoon made mustard, two tablespoons sugar, three tablespoons melted butter, two-thirds cup of vinegar, one-half teaspoon salt Cook as boiled custard in kettle of water. Stir briskly after taking from the fire that it may be smooth.

MRS. C. W. MARSH.

POTATO SALAD.

One dozen cold potatoes sliced thin, one-half teaspoon mustard, one-half teaspoon pepper, one teaspoon salt, butter size of an egg, one-half cup vinegar, one-half cup water, chop celery or a little onion with potatoes. Let the dressing simmer and pour over the potato while hot.
MRS. FRED CARL.

ANOTHER.

Six cold boiled potatoes cut in small cubes. One or two stalks of celery cut in thin slices, put in salad dish, season with salt and pepper, (if you like a little parsley may be used,) then pour over it the dressing.

SALAD DRESSING.

Have a tablespoon of mustard, or half as much, with a little cayenne pepper and mix with it gradually two tablespoons olive oil or melted butter, stir into this a teaspoon of salt, and a tablespoon of sugar, add three beaten eggs and mix thoroughly, then add a cup of milk or cream, and a cup of vinegar. Cook like soft custard.
MRS. E. A. HUBBARD.

VEAL SALAD.

One small teaspoon salt. One large teaspoon mixed mustard, one tablespoon sugar, two raw eggs, butter, size of an egg; beat thoroughly, then add one teacup vinegar. Set in dish of boiling water and stir until it thickens. One and one-half pounds veal and half as much celery.
MISS EUNICE J. MORTON.

WEIGHTS AND MEASURES.

The following is a table of weights and measures.

4 tablespoons, ... 1-2 gill or 1 wine glass or 1-4 cup.
1 tablespoon. . . . . 1-2 ounce.
1 pint, ... 1 pound.
2 gills, ... 1 cup or 1-2 pint.
1 quart of flour, ... 1 pound.
4 cups, ... 1 quart or 1 pound.
1 rounded tablespoon flour, ... 1-2 ounce.
3 cups of corn meal, ... 1 pound.
1 cup of butter, ... 1-2 pound.
1 pint of butter, ... 1 pound.
1 tablespoon of butter, ... 1 ounce.
1 solid pint of chopped meat, ... 1 pound.
10 eggs, ... 1 pound.
2 cups granulated sugar, ... 1 pound.
2 1-2 cups of powdered sugar, ... 1 pound.
1 pint of brown sugar, ... 13 ounces.

BREADS.

"The very staff of life. The comfort of the husband—and the pride of the wife."

POTATO YEAST.

At noon take 2 common sized potatoes, mash them well. Add 1 tablespoon of salt, 1 tablespoon of sugar. Pour over this 1 pint of boiling water, then 1 quart of cold water. Dissolve ½ yeast cake, and let it rise until night. Then make your bread with only the water. Keep the settlings to raise your yeast next time. This will make 4 loaves of bread.

MRS. ERNEST GODIN.

POTATO YEAST.

4 large boiled potatoes, 3 tablespoons flour, 2 tablespoons sugar, 1 tablespoon salt. mix. Pour boiling water over this and strain. When cool add 1 cent's worth brewers' yeast. Bottle.

MRS. ED. GRAVES.

WHEAT BREAD.

1 pint milk, 1 pint water. Warm milk and water. Add 1 tablespoon sugar, 1 teaspoon salt, ½ cent's worth of yeast. Stir in flour sufficient for thin batter. Let it stand until light. Mould in flour until it will not stick, let rise again. Mould into loaves. Makes 2 loaves.

MRS. ED. GRAVES.

BREAD TWICE RAISED.

3 pints milk scalded and cooled, 3 quarts of flour, (or enough for stiff sponge,) 1 tablespoon sugar, 1 teaspoon salt, ½ cake compressed yeast dissolved in a little water. Mix thoroughly and let rise over night. In the morning knead one-half hour, and let rise again. Then mould into loaves, and when light enough bake from fifty minutes to one hour. Three loaves.

MRS. N. D. BILLINGS.

WHEAT BREAD.

1½ quarts warm flour, 1½ pints milk scalded and cooled and well beaten, ½ cake yeast dissolved in little tepid water. Stir together and let rise over night. In the morning add one teaspoon salt, one tablespoon sugar, ½ tablespoon shortening, flour enough to knead. Let rise; when well risen put in two pans and let them rise to twice their size and put in oven to bake.

MISS L. D. PORTER.

GRAHAM BREAD.

2 cups white flour, 2 cups graham flour, 1 cup milk, 3 tablespoons sugar, 1 tablespoon salt, 1 cup water, yeast. One loaf.

MRS. C. W. MARSH.

GRAHAM BREAD.

2 cups of milk, 3 cups graham flour, 1 cup wheat flour, ½ cup molasses, 1 teaspoon of soda, salt. Steam 2 hours and bake one-half hour.

MRS. I. B. LOWELL.

GRAHAM BREAD.

2½ cups graham flour, 1 cup white flour, 1 coffee cup sour milk with teaspoon of soda in it, teaspoon salt, ½ cup molasses, 1 egg, cover with tin and bake in slow oven an hour and a half.

MISS M. E. PHELPS.

GRAHAM CRACKERS.

⅔ cup of butter, 1 cup of sugar, white of one egg well beaten. Add 1 teaspoon cream tartar, ½ teaspoon soda, ½ cup cold water, graham flour enough to knead. Roll thin, cut in squares, prick with a fork and bake in hot oven.

MARIA L. PORTER.

GRAHAM BREAD.

1 pint milk and water, ½ gill molasses, 1 tablespoon brewers' yeast, little salt, flour to stir stiff. Let rise, mould and put in pan. One loaf.

MRS. ED. GRAVES.

GRAHAM BREAD.

2½ cups sour milk, 1 cup molasses, 2 teaspoons soda, 1 teaspoon salt, 3 cups graham, 1 cup wheat flour. Stir in the order named, set to rise for two hours in the loaf pans and bake three fourths of an hour in a medium oven.

MRS. R. M. WOODS.

OAT MEAL BREAD.

2 cups oat meal, pour over 4 cups boiling water at noon, at night stir into this ½ cup of molasses, ½ yeast cake, salt and flour to make it very stiff, about 2 quarts, in the morning place in bread pans and let rise until light.

MRS. R. BILLINGS.

GRAHAM ROLLS.

1 pint sour milk, 1 teaspoon of soda, 1 tablespoon molasses, small half teaspoon salt, graham sufficient for thin batter. Bake in hot gempans.

MRS. C. D. BARDWELL.

BAKED BROWN BREAD.

3 cups graham flour, 1 cup white flour, 1 cup New Orleans molasses, 1 teaspoon of soda dissolved in hot water, 2 cups sour milk, bake one hour and a half in oven not too hot.

ULA GRAVES.

STEAMED BROWN BREAD.

2 cups of milk, 2 cups indian meal, 1½ cups of flour, 1 cup of molasses, 1 teaspoon of soda, steam three hours.

MRS. I. B. LOWELL.

BROWN BREAD.

2 cups of corn meal, 2 cups of white flour, 1 cup of graham flour, ½ cup molasses, 3 cups sour milk or butter milk, 1 heaping teaspoon of soda, scant teaspoon of salt mix and put in covered pail, set in kettle of boiling water, steam for two and a half hours, bake one half hour.

MRS. N. S. HEAFY.

BROWN BREAD.

2½ cups of sour milk, ½ cup molasses 1 teaspoon of salt, 1 teaspoon of soda, 2½ cups Indian meal, 1 cup graham flour, steam three hours.

MARGARET McGRATH.

STEAMED BROWN BREAD.

1 coffee cup molasses, 1 teaspoon soda dissolved in hot water and beaten into molasses, 1 egg, 1 quart sweet milk, 3 cups sifted corn meal, 2 cups graham flour, ½ cup white flour, little salt, steam three and a half hours.

MRS. J. E. PORTER.

BROWN BREAD.

1 cup meal, 2 cups graham, 2 cups milk, ⅔ cup molasses, 1 teaspoon soda, little salt, steam three hours.

MRS. M. H. BURKE.

INDIAN MEAL ROLLS.

2 eggs, ½ cup sugar, 1 large cooking spoon of shortening, ½ cup bolted indian meal, 1 cup sweet milk, 2 cups pastry flour, 2 teaspoons Royal Baking Powder, pinch of salt. Beat eggs, sugar and shortening well together, then add remaining ingredients, beat again and bake in gem pans.

RAISED BISCUIT.

1 quart new milk, ½ cup lard set on stove and when melted add ½ cup sugar, tablespoon of salt. Set aside to cool, when luke warm add 1 cake of compressed yeast dissolved in a little water with small pinch of baking soda, stir as stiff as possible, with well sifted bread flour, then knead well with hands, set in a warm place to rise. In the morning knead down and let it rise again. When light mould into biscuit, let it rise again and bake in rather hot oven.

GEMS.

1 cup of milk, 1 egg, 1½ cups flour, ½ cup corn meal, 2 teaspoons baking powder, salt.

MRS. I. B. LOWELL.

RAISED BISCUIT.

2 quarts flour, 1 pint milk, 1 yeast cake, ½ cup lard, 1 tablespoon sugar.

MRS. GEORGE A. BILLINGS.

RYE MUFFINS.

1 cup rye flour, ¼ cup sugar, ½ teaspoon salt, 2 teaspoons baking powder, 1 cup white flour, 1 egg, 1 cup milk.

MRS. CUTLER.

JOHNNY CAKE.

1½ cups butter-milk, ¼ cup sugar, 1 cup flour, 1 cup Indian meal, 1 egg, 1 large teaspoon soda, little salt, nutmeg.

MRS. J. T. FITCH.

JOHNNY CAKE.

2 cups butter-milk, 1 cup molasses, 1 teaspoon soda, ½ teaspoon salt, 2 cups Indian meal, 2 cups wheat flour.

MRS. D. W. WELLS.

RAISED GRIDDLE CAKE.

1 quart milk scalded, ½ yeast cake, 1 tablespoon sugar, 1 teaspoon salt, flour to make a thin batter. In the morning add ½ teaspoon soda.

MRS. A. L. BARDWELL.

WHEAT ROLLS.

2 cups flour, 2 tablespoons sugar, butter size of egg, ⅔ teaspoon soda, 1½ teaspoons cream tartar. The above worked together with the hands. Then add 1 egg, and milk enough for thick batter. Bake quickly in hot pans.

MRS. C. D. BARDWELL.

NEWPORT ROLLS.

2 eggs, 1 cup milk, 2 tablespoons sugar, 2 teaspoons baking powder, butter size of an egg, 2 cups flour.

MRS. FRED PEASE.

GERMAN SPONGE.

Scald 1½ cups sweet milk, when cool add ½ cup sugar, ¾ yeast cake, 1 beaten egg, flour for batter. When risen, work in with hand ½ cup butter and flour to make soft dough, which can be patted in baking pan. This will make two loaves in jelly tins. When risen, bake quickly, and while hot spread butter on the top, and sprinkle over the whole a little cinnamon and sugar.

MRS. C. M. BARTON.

FRENCH ROLLS.

Stir 1 pint of scalded milk into 3 pints of flour, add ½ cup of lard and ½ cup of sugar. When cold add ½ cup of yeast.

MRS. J. D. PORTER.

WHEAT MUFFINS.

¼ cup butter, ¼ cup sugar, 1 cup milk, pinch of salt, 1½ cups flour or about as thick as cake, 2 teaspoons baking powder.

MRS. J. D. BROWN.

PARKER HOUSE ROLLS.

At night take 2 quarts of flour, rub in 3 tablespoons of lard. Make a hole in middle and put in 1 pint of cold milk, ½ cup yeast, 3 tablespoons sugar, 1 egg and 1 teaspoon of salt. Let stand until morning without mixing. Then mix and when risen cut into rolls. When very light bake quickly.

MRS. C. M. BARTON.

BREAKFAST MUFFINS.

½ cup sugar, 2 teaspoons butter, 1 cup milk, 1 teaspoon soda, little salt, 2½ cups flour, at last stir in 1 egg.

MRS. J. CARL.

BUNS.

3 cups milk, 1 cup sugar, 4 tablespoons yeast, flour enough for batter. Rise over night. Add 1 cup sugar, 1 cup butter, nutmeg, raisins and flour. Raise again. When baked rub over with molasses and cream.

MARY E. BRIGGS.

MUFFINS.

1 cup of sugar, 2 eggs, 1 cup milk, 2½ cups flour, 1 teaspoon cream tartar, ½ teaspoon soda, butter size of an egg.

MARY E. BRIGGS.

PARKER HOUSE ROLLS.

1 pint of milk, ½ cup of butter, ½ cup of sugar, 1 yeast cake, 1 teaspoon of salt, 2 quarts of flour. Scald the milk, add butter to milk, while warm, when cool add sugar, yeast, salt and flour. Let rise until morning, then mould a few moments, again at noon the same, roll out, cut with a round cookie cutter, spreak ½ with melted butter, and turn the other over it Let rise until time to bake for tea. Quick oven.

MRS. F. H. BARDWELL.

BAKING POWDER BISCUIT.

1 quart of flour, 1 pint milk, 2 teaspoons baking powder, little salt. Drop with a spoon into muffin rings.

MRS. D. W. WELLS.

ROLLS.

1 quart sifted flour, 1 tablespoon butter rubbed in flour, 1 tablespoon sugar, 1 teaspoon salt, ½ yeast cake, nearly a pint of milk scalded and cooled. Mix as soft as you can work. Set to rise at nine o'clock in the morning, and at noon stir down, (not mould.) At four or five o'clock roll out ¾ of an inch thick and put melted butter on each and lap together. Rise till light and bake quickly.

MRS. W. H. BELDEN.

TOP OVERS.

2 cups flour, 2 cups milk, 2 eggs, salt, 2 tablespoons melted butter. This makes two dozen. Beat eggs thoroughly, add salt, butter, milk and flour. Bake in hot gem pan in hot stove.

MRS. J. E. PORTER.

WHEAT GEMS.

2 cups water, ½ cup milk, 3 cups entire wheat flour, little salt. Heat gem pans very hot on top of stove fill even full with batter, and place on grate of hot oven, let it remain ten minutes then bake quickly thirty minutes on bottom of the oven.

MRS. DAVID BILLINGS.

PARKER HOUSE ROLLS.

2 quarts of flour, 1 large spoonful of lard rubbed with the flour, put in deep pan and make a hole in the middle. Take a pint of cold boiled milk, ½ a cup of yeast, ½ a cup of sugar mixed, put into the hole and not stir, let it stand over night, stir all together with a spoon and let it remain until after noon, then knead into biscuits, let them stand until quite light or take these ingredients and use them in the ordinary way.

MISS A. LYMAN.

POP OVERS OR BREAKFAST CAKES.

1 egg, 1 cup of flour, 1 cup of milk, little salt, makes one dozen, bake in hot gem pans, in quick oven. Bake twenty minutes.

MRS. H. HUBBARD.

BREAKFAST POCKET BOOKS.

1 quart of warm water or milk, 2 eggs, 3 teaspoons sugar, 1 cup of yeast, 4 tablespoons melted butter. Add flour to make a sponge and set to rise, when risen work over and set to rise again. When light dissolve and add a piece of soda size of a bean, roll out, spread the surface with butter, cut in square and double over to form a pocket book shape, and put them in a pan. Let stand until light, and bake.

MRS. SAMUEL BILLINGS.

PAN CAKES.

1 pint new milk, 2 eggs, 1/2 teaspoon soda, little salt and flour to stiffen, mix well and fry in hot lard.

POP OVERS.

2 cups flour, 2 large cups milk, 2 eggs, small teaspoon salt, makes one dozen. Add a little milk to flour and the rest gradually, and eggs thoroughly beaten, the last thing. Bake in hot oven.

MRS. B. M. WOODS.
MRS. FRED PEASE.
MISS LIZZIE PORTER.

SALLY LUNN.

1 quart flour, 1 tablespoon butter, 3 tablespoons sugar, 2 eggs, 2 teacups milk, 2 teaspoons cream tartar, 1 teaspoon soda, small teaspoon salt.

MRS. N. D. BILLINGS.

GREEN CORN GRIDDLE CAKES.

Grate 1 dozen ears of corn, add to this 1 cup of sifted pastry flour, 1 cup milk, $\frac{1}{2}$ teaspoon salt, 1 teaspoon sugar. Pinch of black pepper and the beaten yolks of 2 eggs. Beat well, stir in the beaten whites, and 2 teaspoons baking powder. If canned corn is used, 1 egg will do for the above receipt.

MRS. A. L. BARDWELL.

CORN FRITTERS.

1 dozen ears of corn grated, 4 eggs, $\frac{1}{4}$ cup of flour, little salt. Fry in hot fat.

MRS. M. N. BURKE.

GOOD CORN BREAD.

Two cups Indian corn, and a cup wheat,
One cup sour milk, one cup sweet,
One good egg that well you beat;
A half cup molasses too,
One half cup sugar add there to
With one spoon of butter (new,)
Salt and soda each one spoon
Mix up quickly and bake it soon,
Then you will have corn bread complete,
Best of all corn bread you meet
It will make your boys eyes shine
If he is like that boy of mine,
If you have a dozen boys
To increase your house hold joys
Double then this rule I should
And you will have two corn cakes good.
When you have nothing nice for tea
This the very thing will be.
All the men that I have seen
Say that its of all the cakes the queen;
Good enough for any king
That a husband home may bring.

PUDDINGS AND SAUCES.

"The proof of the pudding lies in the eating"

TIREBOT CREAM PUDDING.

PINK PORTION.

1 pint cream whipped, 3 eggs, whites beaten, speck of gelatine to hold it, sweeten to taste and flavor with strawberry.

WHITE PORTION

1 pint cream whipped, 3 eggs whites beaten, speck of gelatine, sweeten and flavor with lemon.

YELLOW PORTION.

1 pint rich milk, 6 eggs yolks, gelatine enough to stiffen, sweeten and flavor with vanilla, this can be served with a border of jelly cut in fancy shapes

SARAH McHUGH.

BAKED APPLE DUMPLING.

1 quart of flour, 1 heaping tablespoon of lard, 1 teaspoon soda, 2 teaspoons cream tartar, 1 large coffee cup of milk. Roll and bake one-half hour. Bake apples in dish fifteen minutes before laying on crust. Sauce for above, 1 cup of sugar, 2 tablespoons of butter, 1 teaspoon of flour beaten together, $\frac{1}{2}$ cup of boiling water. Flavor and boil until clear.

MRS. N. D. BILLING.

BAKED SUET PUDDING.

1 cup of suet chopped fine, 2½ cups of flour, 1 cup raisins, 1 cup currants, 1 small cup molasses, ½ teaspoon of nutmeg, 1 teaspoon cinnamon, 2 teaspoons cream tartar, 1 teaspoon soda. Bake one hour in a moderate oven.

SAUCE.

1 cup of sugar, ½ cup of butter, 1 egg all well beaten, 1 tablespoon water, then heat to a scald; when cool flavor to taste.

MRS. J. H. HOWARD.

SNOW PUDDING.

½ box gelatine, 1 pint boiling water, 3 lemons (juice only) 2 cups of sugar, 4 eggs (whites). Soak gelatine in a cup of cold water one-half hour then add the boiling water, the juice of the lemons, the sugar strain and set away to cool. When it begins to cool beat with an egg beater until quite stiff, then add the beaten whites of the eggs. Put in a mould to cool. When cool turn into dish. Serve with boiled custard, made with yolks of the eggs.

MRS. E. B. DICKINSON.

CREAM TAPIOCA.

3 tablespoons tapioca soaked over night, 1 quart of milk, 4 eggs, yolks, 1 cup sugar, 3 tablespoons of prepared cocoanut. Boil milk and tapioca in double boiler half an hour. Add yolks, sugar and cocoanut beaten together and boil ten minutes longer. Beat white to a stiff froth with 3 tablespoons powdered sugar, spread over the top sprinkle with cocoanut and brown in the oven.

MRS. E. B. DICKINSON.

BAKED INDIAN PUDDINGS.

Scald 1 quart milk, 1 cup Indian meal, 1 teacup sugar, 1 teaspoon cinnamon, ½ teaspoon salt. Wet the meal in cold milk, stir into the boiling milk, add the sugar, cinnamon and salt, pour the batter into a 2 quart dish and fill with cold milk, mix, and bake four or five hours.

MRS. FRED CARL.

DELICATE INDIAN PUDDING.

1 quart milk, 2 large tablespoons Indian meal, 1 cup sugar, 3 eggs, scald the milk, add the meal, cook ten minutes and remove from the fire, add the eggs and sugar and stir all together and bake slowly three-quarter of an hour. To be eaten with cream.

MISS NELLIE WHALEN.

CHOCOLATE PUDDING.

1 pint stale bread crumbs, 1 quart milk, 2 squares chocolate, 3 tablespoons sugar, 1 tablespoon hot water, 4 eggs. Soak crumbs in milk one hour, then mash fine, cut chocolate fine into a sauce pan, add 3 tablespoons of sugar and 1 tablespoon hot water, when melted add the milk and bread. Beat the yolks of 4 eggs and the white of one, add 2 more tablespoons of sugar and turn into the mixture. Pour into a buttered dish and bake forty minutes. Cover with a meringue made from the remaining whites of the eggs. Serve with whipped cream.

MRS. C. L. GRAVES.

GRAHAM PUDDING.

1 cup molasses, 1 cup milk, 1 cup raisins, 2 cups graham flour, ½ teaspoon soda, 1 egg. (Steam two hours.)

SAUCE.

Mix with 1 cup cream whipped and sweetened, the beaten white of 1 egg.

MRS. C. A. JONES.

CHOCOLATE PUDDING.

1 pint cream, 1 cup milk, 1/2 cup sugar, 1/2 box gelatine soaked in the milk, 1 square of chocolate. Whip the cream to a stiff froth, melt chocolate and sugar together with a teaspoon of hot water stir gelatine into this mixture and let it cool, then add whipped cream beat all together and put in mould. Serve with cream and sugar.

MARGARET McGRATH.

CORN STARCH PUDDING.

1 quart milk, take out enough to wet 3 tablespoons corn starch, 2 eggs well beaten, 1/2 cup sugar. Boil milk then add beaten eggs, sugar, corn starch and a little salt, flavor with vanilla. Serve with hard sauce.

SAUCE.

1/2 cup butter beaten to a cream, 1 cup sugar. Season with nutmeg.

MRS. R. M. WOODS.

JUDGE PETER'S PUDDING.

3/4 box of gelatine, 2 oranges, (juice only,) 9 dates, 6 figs, two bananas, 2 English walnuts. Dissolve the gelatine in 1/2 pint cold water, let it stand one hour then add 1/2 pint boiling water, 2 lemons, (juice) 2 cups of sugar. Strain and let cool. The jelly must be almost cold before adding the fruit; which has been cut fine. Pour into a fancy dish and serve with whipped cream.

MRS. C. A. JONES.

BREAD PUDDING.

1 pint bread crumbs, 1 quart milk, 1 cup of sugar, 3 eggs (yolks,) piece of butter size of an egg raisins, stirred in dish together and baked. Put layer of jelly over the top after baking, beat the whites of 3 eggs and 1/3 cup of sugar into a meringue. Brown in the oven.

MISS EMMA A. WAITE.

RICE PUDDING.

3 tablespoons (even) rice, 1 quart of milk, $\frac{1}{2}$ cup of sugar, raisins. Bake until the rice is soft, about three hours in a slow oven. Serve cold.

MISS E. SHATTUCK.

PRUNE PUDDING.

White of 3 eggs, 1 teacup stewed prunes, cut in small pieces, 3 tablespoons sugar, 2 teaspoons vanilla. Take the whites of the eggs beaten very stiff with the sugar then whip in the prunes, then add vanilla, put in a buttered dish and bake until brown. Serve with whipped cream and sugar.

MISS EUNICE MORTON.

PRUNE PUDDING.

3 well beaten eggs, $\frac{2}{3}$ cup sugar, 1 cup stewed prunes, 1 pint milk, 1 heaping tablespoon corn starch. Heat the milk to boiling point, stir in the corn starch rubbed smooth in a little cold milk, let this come to a boil, add the prunes and pour into a pudding dish and bake fifteen minutes. Serve with cream.

MRS. D. W. WELLS.

HUCKLEBERRY PUDDING.

3 eggs, 1 cup milk, 1 tablespoon melted butter, 1 pint flour, 3 teaspoons baking powder, 1 pint huckleberries, a little salt. Boil one an one-half hours. Sauce, butter and sugar.

E. A. WAITE.

QUAKING PUDDING.

1 quart milk, 6 eggs, 2 tablespoons butter (warm for buttering the mold,) 1 quart of stale bread cut in thin slices (slivered,) $\frac{1}{2}$ cup dry currants, 1 cup seeded raisins, $\frac{1}{2}$ teaspoon salt, 3 tablespoons sugar, $\frac{1}{4}$ nutmeg. Measure the bread after it is cut, packed solid into a quart measure, butter a 3 quart bowl thoroughly, sprinkle the bottom and sides with currants, lay bread in layers, raisins between layers, and bread on top. Beat eggs, sugar, salt, and nutmeg, add milk and pour over bread. Put in cool place for three hours, steam in a steamer one and one quarter hours. Serve with a creamy sauce made as follows:—

SAUCE.

$\frac{1}{2}$ cup of butter, 1 cup powdered sugar, $\frac{1}{4}$ cup cream or milk, 1 teaspoon vanilla or lemon. Beat butter to a cream adding sugar gradually, beating all the time, when light and creamy, add the flavoring and a little at a time the cream. When all is beaten smooth place the bowl in a basin of hot water until smooth and creamy.

MISS BERTHA THAYER.

STEAM PUDDING.

1 cup sweet milk, $\frac{1}{2}$ cup sugar, $\frac{1}{2}$ cup molasses, 3 cups flour, 1 teaspoon each cinnamon, cloves, soda. Add either raisins or berries. Grease a pail or mold into which put the above. Cover tightly. Steam two hours.

SAUCE.

4 tablespoons boiling milk, 1 egg, 1 cup sugar. Beat egg and sugar together, add to the milk.

MRS. ARTHUR JENNY.

COTTAGE PUDDING.

✗ 1 egg, 1 scant cup of milk, 1 cup of sugar, 2 cups of flour, 2 teaspoons baking powder, 1 tablespoon melted butter. Serve with

SAUCE.

A ½ cup of butter, ⅔ cup of sugar beaten to a cream, 1 teaspoon flour, 1 cup hot water, cook over tea-kettle, juice and rind of 1 lemon.

MRS. ARTHUR CURTIS.

KINGSLEY PUDDING.

1 quart milk, ⅓ box gelatine, 4 eggs, yolks. Cook these together, then add beaten whites, sweeten and flavor to taste Just before it begins to stiffen add 1 dozen macaroons and 1 dozen cocoanut balls. Serve with whipped cream.

SARAH McHUGH.

GRAHAM PUDDING.

1½ cups of graham flour, 1 cup of sweet milk, 1 cup chopped raisins, 1 cup molasses, ½ teaspoon soda, 1 teaspoon cloves and cinnamon. Steam two hours. Serve with whipped cream.

MRS. F. H. BARDWELL.

SWEET CORN PUDDING.

1 pint of sweet corn pulp, 2 eggs, 1½ pints of milk, 1 tablespoon of butter, ½ cup of sugar, raisins if you like.

M. A. MORTON.

BERRY PUDDING.

1 egg, ½ cup sugar, 1 cup buttermilk, 1 teaspoon soda, little salt, 2 cups berries, flour to make a stiff cake, then pour into a 2 quart pan, cover, and boil two hours. Serve with sweetened sauce.

MRS. R. HUBBARD.

CUSTARD SOUFFLE PUDDING.

1 pint milk, ½ cup flour, ½ cup sugar. Stir all together, cook in double boiler until it thickens, then add a small piece of butter. When cool add 4 eggs, whites and yolks beaten separately. Then bake three-quarters of an hour in a pan of water. Serve immediately from the oven with following.

EGG SAUCE.

1 cup of sugar, ½ cup of butter beaten to a cream, 2 eggs beaten together and added to the sugar and butter. Flavor with lemon or vanilla.

MRS. F. H. BARDWELL.

APPLE PUDDING.

Peel, core and slice apples sufficient to fill a baking dish. Butter the dish thickly, and put in the apples in layers alternately with stale cake crumbs and a little melted butter. 2 tablespoons of melted butter to a pint of apples. Let the last layer be a thick one of cake crumbs, then put in a moderately hot oven, until apples are tender, then beat together 2 eggs, 2 tablespoons sugar, more if apples are very tart. Add 1 cup of cream, pour it over the pudding. Return to the oven until the pudding is a rich golden color. Serve with cream.

MRS. B. M. WARNER.

CARAMEL PUDDING.

2 cups sugar, melted, care must be taken not to burn, ½ cup hot water added to sugar, 1 quart milk boiled, 8 eggs, yolks only, 1 tablespoon cornstarch, salt to taste. When cooked add the caramel. Make a meringue of the whites of the eggs and brown in the oven. Serve with whipped cream flavored lightly with vanilla.

SARAH McHUGH.

ORANGE PUDDING.

1 package of minute gelatine, 1 pint boiling water, 1 cup sugar, 3 oranges. Dissolve the gelatine in the pint of boiling water, add the sugar and stir well, add grated rind and juice of the oranges, and stir all together, when cold pour over 1 cup whipped cream, flavor with extract of orange.

MISS NELLIE ORMONDE.

ORANGE PUDDING.

6 oranges, 1 cup sugar, 1 pint milk, 3 eggs. Scald the milk, add the yolks of three eggs well beaten, stir constantly. As soon as it thickens add to the oranges which have been cut into small pieces. Beat the whites of the eggs to a stiff froth, adding 1 tablespoon sugar to each egg. Spread on top and set in the oven to brown.

MRS. C. L. WARNER.

PINEAPPLE PUDDING.

½ cup of minute tapioca, 1 cup sugar, 1 pint water, 2 lemons, 2 eggs, (whites,) 1 pint pineapple. Boil the tapioca in the water until clear. Add the juice of the lemons, add sugar and stir in the beaten whites of the eggs, add the pineapple cut in inch pieces. Serve cold with sweet cream.

MRS. CHARLES GRAVES.

INDIAN PUDDING.

2 quarts of milk, 1 cup Indian meal, 1 cup molasses, 2 eggs, ½ teaspoon salt. Scald meal in 1 quart of milk. Add the rest of the milk, molasses, eggs and salt. Put in pudding dish. Cover the top with small bits of butter and bake three hours.

MRS. I. B. LOWELL.

ENGLISH PLUM PUDDING.

1½ pounds seeded raisins, 1 ounce candied lemon peel chopped, 1 ounce candied orange peel chopped, ½ ounce bitter almonds, 1 pound suet chopped fine. Mix the suet with 1 quart of sifted bread crumbs. Add the raisins, peels and almonds, and the grated rind of a fresh lemon, 1 teaspoon nutmeg, 1 teaspoon cinnamon, 1 pound light brown sugar, 8 eggs beaten very light. Add the sugar, and stir into fruit mixture. Then add ½ cup of strong coffee. Put in a well greased mold and steam three hours. Serve with a hard sauce.

M. A. MORTON.

SUET PUDDING.

1 cup chopped raisins, 1 cup suet chopped fine, 1 cup molasses, 1 cup milk, 1 teaspoon soda, 1 teaspoon spices, all kinds, 3 cups of flour. Stir in the order named and steam three hours. Serve with

SAUCE.

2 eggs, whites only, 4 tablespoons sugar. Flavor with vanilla.

MRS. CHLOE MORTON.

IMPERIAL RICE PUDDING.

1 teacup rice boiled soft, 3 tablespoons butter, nutmeg, sugar, salt to taste, 1 quart creamy milk, ¼ pound raisins, ¼ pound currants, ¼ pound citron and candied cherries. Serve with English cream sauce made as follows:—1 pint rich milk, 6 eggs, yolks beaten, and add to the boiling milk. Sweeten to taste. Flavor with vanilla. Beat until cold.

SARAH McHUGH.

CREME—DIPLOMATE.

1 quart rich cream, well whipped, 6 eggs, whites only, beaten stiff, ¼ box gelatine, soaked and strained Sweeten and flavor with vanilla. 2 dozen lady fingers, ½ dozen macaroons arranged in a mold. Just before pouring in the cream, add ½ pound candied fruits which have been soaked.

SARAH McHUGH.

CRACKER PUDDING.

1 quart of milk, 4 crackers rolled fine, 2 eggs, yolks only, salt. Bake thirty minutes. When nearly cool make a meringue of whites of eggs and ¾ cup of sugar. Return to oven and brown quickly.

MRS. I. B. LOWELL.

PUDDING SAUCES.
WHIPPED CREAM.

1 coffee cup cream, 2 eggs, (whites,) 2 tablespoons sugar, ½ teaspoon flavoring extract. Beat all together with an egg beater until stiff. A good sauce for many kinds of cake or pudding.

MRS. B. M. WARNER.

PUDDING SAUCE.

1 egg (yolk,) 1 cup sugar, 2 tablespoons flour, 1 cup boiling water, butter size of an egg. Beat the sugar and yolk of the egg with a little water together, then add the flour, then the cup of boiling water also butter. Let this boil a few moments and pour it on the well beaten white of an egg and stir very lightly. Add 2 teaspoons vanilla.

MRS. P. J. BOYLE.

PUDDING SAUCE.

1 egg well beaten with 1½ cup of sugar. Pour on this 2 tablespoons of boiling milk. Beat until it is light. Flavor.

MRS. E. A. HUBBARD.

PUDDING SAUCE.

1 cup sugar, ⅓ cup butter, 1 egg, 1 lemon, juice, 3 tablespoons boiling water. Cream the butter and sugar, and beat in the egg whipped light, then the lemon. Add a little at a time the boiling water. Set in the top of the tea-kettle till it is very hot, stirring constantly. It should be the consistency of rich cream.

MRS. J. S. WELLS.

RICE PUDDING.

1 tea-cup rice, boiled in 2 cups water, add 1 quart milk, boil until soft. Butter ½ size of egg, 6 eggs, salt. Beat yolks and whites separate, the sugar with the yolks stir into rice, also salt and butter Return to fire 2 or 3 minutes, being careful not to burn. Pour into buttered dish. Beat the 6 whites and 6 tablespoons sugar to a stiff froth, flavor with lemon, lay it over the pudding in folds like a turban, set in the oven to brown.

PIES.

No soil upon earth is so dear to our eyes,
As the soil we first stirred into terrestrial pies.
(O. W. Holmes.)

PIE CRUST.

4 teacups flour, 1 heaping cup lard, 1 teaspoon salt, mix lightly with ice water. Add one teaspoon baking powder to flour.

MRS. A. F. CURTIS.

PUFF PASTE.—(VERY NICE.)

1 quart sifted flour, 1 teaspoon baking powder, 1 teaspoon salt, 1 teacup lard, very cold, rubbed in fine, just enough ice water and the beaten white of an egg to make a stiff dough. Roll in sheets, make three parts to a cup of butter, roll out three times and set on ice. The egg may be omitted.

SARAH McHUGH

NICE MINCE PIE.

1 bowl of chopped meat, 1 bowl chopped suet, 3 bowls chopped apples, 1 bowl molasses, 1 bowl sugar 1 bowl cider or sweet pickle juice, 7 teaspoons cinnamon, 5 teaspoons cloves, 2 nutmegs, raisins. Any fruit you like, salt and pepper to taste.

MRS. S. G. HUBBARD.

MINCE MEAT FOR PIES.

1 cup chopped meat, 1½ cups raisins, 1½ cups currants, 1½ cups brown sugar, 1 cup granulated sugar, 3 cups chopped apples, 1 cup meat liquor, 2 teaspoons salt, 2 teaspoons cinnamon, ½ teaspoon powdered cloves, 1 lemon, grated rind and juice, 1 cup boiled cider or sweet pickle juice, mix in the order given. Cook in a porcelain kettle until the apples and raisins are soft. Meat from the vein or lower part of the round that has a little fat and no bone is the best for pie meat. Meat should be boiled until tender before chopped.

MRS. R. M. WOODS.

STAWBERRY CREAM PIE.

1 pint milk, 4 eggs (yolks), 1 teaspoon cornstarch, sweeten, 1 large cup berries or one can. Put on a layer of jam before covering with a meringue.

SARAH McHUGH.

CREAM PIE.

1 pint milk, ¾ cup sugar, 2 eggs (yolks), 1 tablespoon flour. Scald the milk in a double boiler, then add eggs and sugar, butter the size of an egg, then the flour. Have ready a nicely baked crust in a deep pie plate. Beat the whites of the eggs to a stiff froth add 2 tablespoons sugar, put on top, place in the oven until a delicate brown. Very nice for a change with 2 tablespoons of cocoa in the cream.

ULA GRAVES.

CREAM PIE.

3 eggs, 8 tablespoons sugar, 1 tablespoon flour, 1½ cups sweet cream, 4 teacups milk, a little salt, and nutmeg. Beat the eggs fast for five minutes, then add sugar and flour and beat five minutes, then add the other ingredients.

MRS. FRED CARL.

CREAM PIE.

½ cup cream, 1 cup milk, 1 tablespoon flour, 1 egg, 1 cup sugar, vanilla. Mix flour and milk, cook in a double boiler, remove from stove, add the other ingredients. Bake with two crusts.

MRS. WM. BILLINGS.

SQUASH PIE.

1 quart scalded milk, (its better part cream) 1 pint sifted squash, 2 cups sugar, 2 tablespoons flour, (stirred into the squash) 3 eggs, flavor with nutmeg. This makes two large or four small pies.

MRS. EDWARD ELDRIDGE.

CRANBERRY PIE.

3 large cups cranberries, 3 cups sugar, ½ cup raisins, 2 cups boiling water, 1 large tablespoon cornstarch. Chop berries and raisins, add sugar and water, then add dissolved cornstarch. Boil until it thickens a little. Enough for three pies.

CARRIE W. HOLT.

LEMON MERINGUE PIE.

2 lemons, 1½ cups sugar, 1 tablespoon cornstarch, 2 cups boiling water, 3 eggs, (yolks), butter size of a walnut. Stir well together the lemons, sugar and cornstarch, add the water. Cook and add the yolks of the eggs, also butter. Pour into a baked crust spread with three spoons currant jelly. And cover with a meringue of three eggs.

SARAH McHUGH.

RHUBARD PIE.

1 cup chopped rhubard, 1 cup sugar, 1 egg well beaten, 1 tablespoon flour. Bake with two crusts.

MRS. R. BILLINGS.

LEMON PIE.

1 lemon, (grated rind and juice) 2 eggs, (yolks) 1 cup sugar. Cook in a double boiler, when cool add the well beaten whites of the eggs. Put in a crust already baked, and put in the oven to brown.

MRS. D. F. SHATTUCK.

MOCK MINCE PIE.

1 cup chopped raisins, 1½ cups sugar, 1½ cups molasses, 2 cups water, ½ cup vinegar, 8 crackers rolled fine, 1 teaspoon cinnamon, ½ cup butter, a little salt and nutmeg. Makes four pies.

MRS. WM. BILLINGS.

SQUASH PIE.

1½ cups sifted squash, 1 pint cream, 2 cups sugar, 4 eggs, 1 pint milk, cinnamon. This quantity makes four pies.

MRS. T. GRAVES.

CREAM PIE.

1¼ cups milk, 4 tablespoons sugar, 2 tablespoons flour, 2 eggs. Flavor with vanilla.

MRS. ERNEST GODIN.

CUSTARD PIE.

4 eggs, (well beaten) 2 tablespoons flour, 2 small cups sugar, (beat for five minutes) 1 quart milk beaten in slowly. Have the oven hot enough to brown quickly then close the dampers and bake slowly. Makes two pies.

MRS. A. H. GRAVES.

CHOCOLATE PIE.

8 tablespoons grated chocolate, 1 quart boiling water, 4 tablespoons flour or cornstarch, 12 tablespoons sugar. Boil like custard, fill pies, bake, put meringue on top. Makes two pies.

MRS. A. H. GRAVES.

COCOANUT PIE.

3 eggs ½ cup shredded cocoanut (soaked in 1 pint milk) 1 cup sugar, small piece butter, bake with one crust. Be sure and watch while baking If desired you can use less eggs and use 1 tablespoon flour.

MRS. C. D. BARDWELL.

CHICKEN PIE.

Parboil two chickens, make a paste using three teaspoons of baking powder to one quart of sifted flour, wetting the paste with sweet cream, a little salt. Remove skin and bones, placing the chicken in dish, salt and pepper, small pieces of butter. Add liquor in which the chickens were parboiled, after removing the grease, cover with the paste, having well punctured.

MRS. HENRY HUBBARD.

APPLE PUDDING PIES.

5 cups stewed and strained sour apples, 1 small teacup butter, added while hot, 2 cups sugar, 5 eggs beaten light, 2½ cups cream or rich milk. Make three pies baked with one crust. Less eggs, cream and butter may be used and still be very nice.

MRS. A. F. CURTIS.

RICE PIE.

¼ cup boiled rice, 2 eggs, ⅔ pint milk, ½ cup cream, ⅔ cup sugar, ½ teaspoon salt, butter size of a walnut, ½ cup seeded raisins, nutmeg to taste. Bake with one crust.

MRS. A. S. BROWN.

LEMON PIE.

3 eggs (yolks,) 1 teaspoon flour, 1 cup sugar, 1 lemon, juice and grated rind, 1½ cups milk, pinch of salt. Bake with one crust, when nearly cold cover with a meringue, made of the whites of three eggs, and brown in the oven.

MRS. M. A. MORTON.

PLAIN AND FANCY DESSERTS

"The Smile of the Hostess is the Cream of the Feast."

PINE APPLE CREAM.

Stir 1 pound grated pine apple with 1 cup sugar (ten minutes), ½ box gelatine soaked in ½ cup cold water until soft, then dissolve in ½ cup of boiling water and strain into the pine apple. When cool and lightly stiffened add a pint of whipped cream, put in lightly. The whites of 4 or 5 eggs may be used instead of cream.

MISS CARRIE WARNER.

WHIPPED APPLE CREAM.

1 egg (white) 1 cup strained apple, ¾ cup sugar. Whip until it will not drop from a spoon, pour over it the following; 1 pint milk (in double boiler) let come to a boil, stir into this 2 eggs and the yolk of 1 beaten with ¼ cup sugar and 1 tablespoon corn starch.

MRS. T. GRAVES.

COFFEE BLANC MANGE.

1 pint of coffee, 1 pint of water, 1 cup of sugar, ½ box of gelatine dissolved in little water, let all come to a boil, strain into a mould and cool. Serve with whipped cream, or sugar and cream.

MRS. C. K. MORTON.

TAPIOCA CREAM.

4 large spoonfuls of tapioca, 1 quart of milk, yolks of 4 eggs, 1 cup sugar. Cover tapioca with cold water and soak over night. Set milk on stove to warm. Beat yolks of eggs and sugar together, stir into the warm milk with pinch of salt, then stir in tapioca. Beat whites to a stiff froth and stir into the custard. Flavor with lemon or vanilla.

MRS. G. A. BILLINGS.

PRUNE WHIP.

½ pound prunes, 4 eggs (whites) ½ cup sugar. Soak the prunes over night, in the morning stew until tender with the sugar. Rub through a sieve. Beat the whites of the eggs to a stiff froth, add the sifted prunes, beating well together. Heap upon a platter, and bake in a slow oven fifteen or twenty minutes, allowing the whip to brown delicately. Serve with custard sauce.

SAUCE.

Scald 1 pint of milk, beat the yolks of 4 eggs slightly, add 4 tablespoons sugar and ½ saltspoon of salt, pour on the hot milk and cook in a double boiler until it thickens. When cold flavor with ½ teaspoon vanilla extract.

MISS HELEN SMITH.

CHEESE STRAWS.

Take 1 tablespoon of fine bread crumbs, 3 tablespoons of flour, little salt, 4 tablespoons of grated rich cheese. Add to these the yolk of 1 egg, 1 tablespoon of water, then mix until hard, roll out to about ¼ of an inch thickness, cut into strips and bake in a quick oven until a pale brown.

CHEESE STRAWS.

Chop together 1 cup flour, ⅓ cup butter, 1 salt spoon salt. Mix to a stiff dough roll out very thin, sprinkle with 2 tablespoons cheese, roll out again and sprinkle. Add 1 saltspoon salt, cut in narrow strips and bake in a moderate oven ten or fifteen minutes.

MISS HELEN SMITH.

SHORT CAKE.

1 quart of flour, 3 teaspoons baking powder, salt, and sift several times. Rub in the flour 1 tablespoon butter and 1 of lard. Mix with milk. Take ½ the mixture and roll as large as the pan to be baked in, spread with butter, roll out the other portion, put on top and bake in a quick oven.

MRS. CHARLES JONES.

STRAWBERRY SHORT CAKE.

½ cup butter, 1 quart flour, 2 eggs, little salt, 3 heaping teaspoons baking powder, milk to make thick batter. Rub butter well into flour, add salt and baking powder, then add eggs well beaten. Wet with enough milk to make thick batter. Bake quickly. Split with warm knife. Butter top pieces, spread with layer of strawberries. Serve with crushed berries, sweetened, to which plenty of cream has been added. Pour over the whole whipped cream if wanted very rich.

MRS. ALFRED H. GRAVES.

RASPBERRY TAPIOCA.

4 tablespoons tapioca soaked over night in 1 cup water. Add ½ cup water in the morning and heat in double boiler. When clear, add cup of strained red raspberry juice, (bottled,) 1 cup sugar and juice of small lemon. Pour in small moulds and when set, serve with thin sweet cream.

MISS LUCY WEBBER.

CHOCOLATE BLANC MANGE.

1 quart of milk, 1 ounce of gelatine, 4 tablespoons grated chocolate, 3 eggs. 1 cup sugar. Reserve 1 cup from the quart and soak 1 ounce of gelatine in it. Grate chocolate and dissolve in a little milk, add eggs, whites and yolks separately. Add sugar, flavor with vanilla.

MRS. WM. BILLINGS.

ORANGE CUSTARD.

Separate the whites of 8 eggs from the yolks, setting latter away in a cool place. Add the grated rind and juice of 2 large oranges to the whites, and after beating well add ½ pint of water and set away for an hour. Then beat yolks of eggs add them with one cupful of sugar to the mixture of whites, orange and water, strain into a pitcher and set into a basin of boiling water. Let it boil rapidly stiring the mixture meanwhile until it becomes as thick as heavy cream. Allow the custard to cool, pour into glass cups and set away to get cold.

LUCY WEBBER.

BAKED CUSTARD.

1 quart milk, 4 eggs, 3 large tablespoons sugar. Scald the milk. Beat the eggs thoroughly. Add the sugar. Stir into the milk when hot. Strain into cups or a dish and bake slowly. Pour into cups when cold and flavor.

BOILED CUSTARD.

1 quart rich milk, 4 eggs, 1 cup sugar. Scald the milk, then add eggs and sugar, cook well but do not let it curdle. When cold add 1 teaspoon vanilla.

COFFEE PUFF.

1 pint cream, ⅔ cup powdered sugar, ½ cup cold coffee. Whip cream, when nearly done add sugar, then the coffee slowly. Put it in a pail or mould. Pack in ice and salt; use ⅓ as much salt as ice and let it stand three hours. Before serving dip pail in warm water for a second, then slip from the mould.

MRS. C. K. MORTON.

ANOTHER.

1 pint sweet cream, ½ cup sugar, ½ cup strong coffee. Beat the cream and sugar, add coffee, then pack as for ice cream. Let it remain three hours without stirring.

MRS. FRED CARL.

COFFEE JELLY.

1 box of gelatine, 1½ quarts of coffee. Strain coffee, sweeten slightly, pour into mould, serve with whipped cream.

MISS E. A. WAITE.

PINEAPPLE ICE.

4 cups water, 3 cups sugar, 2 eggs (whites.) Boil together the sugar and water. Add ½ a can grated pineapple. When nearly frozen add whites of the eggs.

LOUISE BARDWELL.

MILK SHERBET.

Juice of 2 lemons, 1 pint of sugar, 1 quart of milk. Do not mix lemon and milk until ready to freeze.

MISS. EUNICE MORTON.

BEATEN CREAM.

Place a bowl in a pan of pounded ice, pour in it 1 pint rich cream beat until stiff. Sift in gently 8 tablespoons powdered sugar and ½ teaspoon vanilla. This may be used for filling to cake, charlotte russe, cream cakes or eclairs.

MILK SHERBET.

1 pint of sugar, juice of 2 lemons, 1 teaspoon of extract of lemon, 1 quart of milk. Mix the extract, sugar, and juice together in freezer, then pour in the milk and freeze at once.

MRS. W. H. BELDEN.

ICE CREAM.

2 quarts milk, 2 cans condensed milk, 1 cup sugar, flavor to taste. This makes 1 gallon.

MRS. R. BILLINGS.

RASPBERRY PUFF.

2 eggs (whites) beaten stiff, ½ cup sugar, ½ cup raspberry jam, all beaten till very stiff. Serve with whipped cream.

MRS. C. W. MARSH.

COFFEE ICE CREAM.

1 cup strong coffee, 1 large cup sugar boiled together until it is a syrup. While hot add a cup of milk and the yolks of 3 eggs well beaten. Take syrup from the fire and pour over the eggs and milk, beating rapidly. Then return to the fire and cook until it begins to thicken. Great care must be taken that it does not curdle. Add 1 pint cream and freeze.

MRS. E. A. WAITE.

CARAMEL ICE CREAM.

4 heaping tablespoons sugar put on the range in a sauce pan, and kept there until it melts, smokes and boils, 2 cups milk boiling. Beat the yolks of 4 eggs and stir into the boiling milk, then add burnt sugar and mix well together Finally add 2 small cups of granulated sugar. Put on ice to cool. Before freezing add 1 pint of cream.

MRS. E. A. WAITE.

VANILLA ICE CREAM.

3 eggs, 1 pint milk, 1 cup sugar, 1 teaspoon vanilla. Make the custard several hours before freezing and add 1 pint sweet cream.

For raspberry ice cream omit the vanilla and add 1 quart berries. Put 1 cup sugar on berries and let stand an hour or two before mashing and setting through the strainer.

MRS. E. A. WAITE.

STRAWBERRY SHERBET.

2 quarts of berries, 1 pint sugar, 1½ pints water, 1 tablespoon gelatine. Mash berries and sugar together, and let stand two hours. Soak gelatine in cold water just enough to cover. Add 1 pint of the water to the berries and strain. Dissolve gelatine in ½ pint of boiling water. Add this to the strained mixture and freeze. Raspberry sherbet the same.

MISS EMMA A. WAITE.

ICE CREAM.

1 quart of milk, 1 cup of sugar, 1 tablespoon of corn starch, 4 eggs. Save out whites of 2 eggs. Make custard. Beat the whites of 2 eggs, and add 2 tablespoons sugar. Stir in the custard just before freezing.

MRS. ANNA ELDRIDGE.

LEMON ICE.

6 lemons, juice of all, and grated rind of 3. 1 large sweet orange, juice and grated rind, 1½ pints of water, 1 pint sugar. Squeeze out every drop of juice and add the rind of the orange, and let stand one-half hour. Strain, squeezing the bag dry; mix in the sugar and then the water. Stir until sugar is entirely dissolved, and then freeze.

MRS. R. M. WOODS.

LEMON ICE.

3 cups sugar, 4 lemons, $\frac{1}{4}$ box gelatine, 1 quart water. Boil sugar and water together, let it cool. Dissolve gelatine in a little cold water, then pour a cup of boiling water over it. Grate the rind of 2 lemons. Freeze same as ice cream. When half frozen add beaten whites of 3 eggs.

MRS. C. D. BARDWELL.

ICE CREAM.

2 quarts sweet milk, 6 eggs, $1\frac{1}{2}$ cups sugar, 1 heaping tablespoon corn starch. When cool add 1 quart sweet cream, sweeten to taste, flavor and freeze. This will make 1 gallon.

MRS. C. M. BARTON.

NUT ICE CREAM.

1 quart cream, 1 coffee cup milk, 1 coffee cup sugar, thoroughly heated. When cold, add 1 tablespoon vanilla and 1 cup English walnuts chopped fine. Freeze.

MISS EUNICE MORTON.

CAKE.

*With weights and measures just and true,
Oven of even heat,
Well buttered tins and quiet nerves,
Success will be complete.*

MACAROONS.

1 teacup pounded blanched almonds, 1 teacup brown sugar, 2 tablespoons flour, 1 egg, (white,) salt.

The white of the egg must be sufficient to moisten so that they can be molded into balls, as large as a walnut. Place them well apart upon buttered white paper, the thinner the paper the better.

MRS. A. M. PECK.

COCOANUT CAKE.

½ cup butter, 2 cups sugar, ½ cup cocoanut, ½ cup milk, 2½ cups flour, 4 eggs, 2 teaspoons baking powder. This make 2 loaves.

MISS M. MILLER.

POP DOODLE.

1 egg, 1 cup sugar, 1 cup milk, 2 scant cups flour, 2 scant teaspoons baking powder. Butter size of a walnut. Bake in a dripping pan, but before putting in the oven, sprinkle sugar and cinnamon on top of batter.

MRS. FRED CARL.

HERMIT CAKES.

1 cup butter, 1½ cups white sugar, 3 eggs, ½ teaspoon soda dissolved in milk, 1 nutmeg, 1 teaspoon each of all kinds of spice, ½ pound currants, ¼ pound citron chopped fine. Mix hard, roll thin, cut like cookies. Will keep nicely.

MRS. W. H. BELDEN.

POUND CAKE.

10 ounces sugar, 10 ounces flour, 8 ounces butter, 5 eggs. Mix the flour and butter, grating the nutmeg in the flour. Froth the whites of the eggs, beat the yolks hard with sugar, add alternately the whites and the butter and flour. Beat hard.

MRS. G. A. BILLINGS.

FILLING FOR CAKE.

2 cups sugar, 1 cup sweet cream. Boil together twenty minutes.

MRS. J. E. PORTER.

BLACK FRUIT CAKE.

3 eggs, 1 cup butter, 1 cup molasses, 1 cup brown sugar, ½ nutmeg, 1 teaspoon each cinnamon and cloves, ½ teaspoon each all-spice and saleratus, 1½ cups currants, 1½ cups raisins. Stir in flour until very stiff.

MRS. J. H. HOWARD.

BLACK OR WEDDING CAKE.

3 pounds raisins, 3 pounds currants, 1½ pounds sugar, 1½ pounds citron, 1½ pounds butter, 1½ pounds flour, 14 eggs, 2 lemons, grated rind, nutmegs, cloves, and all-spice to taste. 1 cup molasses, 3 gills brandy, 1 gill wine, 1 teaspoon soda.

MRS. L. L. PEASE.

WALNUT CAKE.

1½ cups sugar, ½ cup butter, 2 cups flour, ½ cup milk, 4 eggs, (whites only,) 1½ teaspoons baking powder, 1 cup walnut meats.

MISS EMMA WAITE.

CHOCOLATE CAKE.

1 cup sugar, 1 small tablespoon shortening, 1 whole egg or two whites, ⅔ cup milk, 1½ cups flour, 1 teaspoon soda, 2 teaspoons cream tartar. Flavor with vanilla, bake in shallow tins. Frost with boiled frosting flavored with vanilla. Dissolve 2 squares Baker's chocolate, and spread over the top, or make a frosting by taking 2 tablespoons milk and stir it stiff with powdered sugar. Flavor and spread the chocolate over it.

MRS. FRANK JONES.

SPONGE CAKE.

4 eggs, 2 cups flour, 2 cups sugar, 1 lemon, 1 heaping teaspoon baking powder, 1 scant cup cold water, pinch of salt. Beat the yolks and sugar together twenty minutes, adding 3 or 4 tablespoons water and beat five minutes. Add flour and lemon, last of all add whites after they have been well beaten. Stir as little as possible after adding the whites.

MISS E. SHATTUCK.

ANGEL CAKE.

11 eggs, (whites,) 1½ cups sugar, 1 cup pastry flour, 1 teaspoon cream tartar, 1 teaspoon vanilla. Measure the flour after being sifted six times. Sift flour and cream tartar together, beat the whites to a stiff froth, beat the sugar into the eggs, add seasoning and flour, stirring lightly and swiftly. Bake forty minutes in a moderate oven in an ungreased pan.

MRS. E. B. D.

ORANGE CAKE.

½ cup butter, 2 cups sugar, 2 eggs, 1 cup sweet milk, 3 cups flour, 2 teaspoons baking powder. The juice of one orange added last. Bake in layers. Put together with icing and sliced oranges. 2 loaves.

MRS. GREENE.

QUICK LOAF CAKE.

1 cup butter, 2 cups sugar, 2 cups milk, 2 eggs, 2 teaspoons cream tartar, 1 teaspoon soda, 5 cups flour, raisins and spice to taste.

MRS. M. H. BURKE.

SUNSHINE CAKE.

5 eggs, 1 cup of sugar, 1 cup flour, pinch of salt. Boil sugar with just a little water until clear and pour on the whites of the eggs, beaten very stiff, then beat ten or fifteen minutes, add yolks which have been beaten light, then flour sifted 3 times and the juice of a ½ lemon. Bake in ungreased pan forty minutes.

MRS. GEO. BILLINGS.

CREAM PUFFS.

½ cup butter, 1 cup boiling water. Set over stove to boil, 1 cup pastry flour, stir into butter and water while boiling, when cold add 3 well beaten eggs, soda size of a pea, mixed with the flour. Bake on buttered pans, making twelve.

CREAM.

½ pint milk on stove, 1 egg, ½ cup sugar, 4 tablespoons flour, 2 teaspoons lemon. Pour on boiling milk and stir until it thickens. Add extract when cold. Fill the cakes as you want them.

MRS. A. S. BROWN.

PORK CAKE.

¾ of a pound of salt pork without lean or rind, chopped as fine as lard. Pour on ½ pint boiling water. 1 egg, 2 cups sugar, 1 cup molasses, 1 teaspoon soda, 2 cups raisins, 1 cup of currants, citron chopped, nutmeg, all-spice, cloves, cinnamon. Thicken as thick as loaf cake.

MRS. C. E. HUBBARD.

CHOCOLATE CAKE (DEVILS' FOOD.)

½ cup butter, 1½ cups sugar, ½ cup milk, 2 eggs, ¼ cake of chocolate, dissolved in ½ cup of boiling water, 1¾ cups of flour, 2 teaspoons baking powder, 1 teaspoon of vanilla. Bake in 2 layers and cover with icing, putting icing between the layers.

MRS. S. G. HUBBARD.

HALLIGAR CAKE.

1 cup sugar, 2 cups flour, ½ cup milk, ½ cup butter, whites of 4 eggs, 1 teaspoon cream tartar, ½ teaspoon soda.

MRS. D. L. FITZGERALD.

CAKE WITHOUT EGGS.

1 cup sugar, 2 cups sifted flour, 5 tablespoons butter, 1 teaspoon of vanilla or lemon, 2 teaspoons baking powder. Beat thoroughly, good with chocolate frosting.

ULA GRAVES.

COCOANUT CAKE.

1 cup sugar, 1 cup cocoanut, 2 cups flour, ½ cup milk, ½ cup butter, 2 eggs, 2 teaspoons of baking powder, cream, sugar and butter. Add beaten eggs, then milk and lastly flour and baking powder sifted together.

MISS NELLIE WHALEN.

COFFEE CAKE.

1 cup butter, 1 cup strong coffee, 1 cup sugar, 4 cups flour, 1 cup molasses, 1 pound raisins, ¼ pound citron, ½ pound currants, 1 teaspoon soda. 2 teaspoons cream tartar, 1 teaspoon of each of the spices.

MRS. D. L. FITZGERALD.

FIG CAKE.

1½ cups sugar, ½ cup butter, whites of 3 eggs, 1 cup milk, 1 teaspoon soda, 2 teaspoons cream tartar, 2½ cups of flour. Bake in 3 or 4 tins. Filling:—½ pound figs, chopped fine, ¾ cup of water, 1 cup of sugar. Boil on stove until like jelly, then spread between cake.

MRS. F. H. BARDWELL.

COMPOSITION CAKE.

3½ cups of flour, 2 cups of sugar, ½ cup of butter, 3 eggs, 1 cup of sweet milk, 1 teaspoon cream tartar, ½ teaspoon soda. Spice and fruit.

MISS A. P. LYMAN.

CHOCOLATE CAKE.

1 square Baker's chocolate, ¼ cup milk, yolk of 1 egg, 2 tablespoons sugar, 1 teaspoon vanilla. Cook like boiled custard and stir into cake part. Cake:— 1 cup sugar, ½ cup milk, 1½ cups flour, ¼ cup butter, 1 egg, 1½ teaspoons baking powder.

MISS M. L. WAITE.

CREAM SPONGE CAKE.

Break 2 eggs in a cup, fill with cream, 1 cup of sugar, 1½ cups of flour, 1 teaspoon of cream tartar, ½ teaspoon of soda. Flavor with vanilla.

MRS. E. M. GRAVES.

FRUIT CAKE.

1 pound of flour, ¾ pound of sugar, ¾ pound of butter, 2 pounds of fruit, ¼ cup of molasses, ½ cup of strong coffee, 6 eggs, 1 teaspoon cloves, ½ teaspoon cinnamon, ¼ teaspoon nutmeg, ¼ teaspoon soda.

RAISED CAKE.

3 cups of milk, 2 cups of sugar, 1 cup of yeast. Put together in the order given. Add flour to make a batter as stiff as can be with a spoon. In the morning add 2 cups sugar, 2 cups butter, ½ cup lard, 2 eggs. 2 nutmegs, raisins. Work well with hands until very light. Put in pans and let rise again. Makes 3 large or 4 small loaves.

RAISED CAKE.

1 cup sugar, 1 cup milk, ⅔ cup yeast. If compressed yeast is used add water enough to make ⅔ cup. Make stiff and stir with a spoon. Let stand until morning, then add 1 cup sugar, 1 cup butter, 2 eggs. Give all a good beating, then add 1 cup floured raisins and other fruit if desired. This makes 2 large loaves.

ANNA C. DEA.

RAISED DOUGH CAKE.

1 cup of raised dough, 1 cup of sugar, ½ cup of butter, ½ cup of milk, 1 cup of flour, 1 cup of raisins, 1 egg, 1 teaspoon of cream tartar, ½ teaspoon of soda sifted in flour. Spice to taste.

MRS. E. ELDRIDGE.

SPONGE CAKE.

2 eggs well beaten, 1¼ cups sugar, 1 teaspoon baking powder, 2 cups flour. Beat together thoroughly. Add ½ cup of cold water.

ANNA E. HARRIS.

RAISED LOAF CAKE.

2 cups sugar, 1 cup shortening, (half butter and half lard,) 3 cups of milk, 1 cup of yeast or 1 compressed yeast cake. Stir in flour sufficient for a stiff batter, and let rise over night. In the morning add 2 cups sugar, 1 cup of shortening, 2 eggs, 1 small teaspoon soda, nutmeg, cinnamon, 3 cups raisins, 1 cup currants, 1 cup citron. Makes 4 loaves.
MRS. T. GRAVES.

LEMON CAKE.

4 eggs, 1 cup sugar, 3 tablespoons sweet milk, 3 tablespoons melted butter, 3 teaspoons baking powder, 1 cup flour. Sauce:—1 lemon, (juice and grated rind,) 1 cup cold water, 1 cup sugar, 1 egg, 1 tablespoon corn starch. Beat lemon rind and egg together, add sugar and lemon juice, dissolve cornstarch in cold water. Cook in a double boiler until it jellies.
MRS. JOSEPH STODDARD.

DELICATE CAKE.

1 1/2 cups sugar, 1/2 cup butter, 1/2 cup milk, 2 cups flour, 2 teaspoons baking powder, whites of six eggs, beaten very stiff, 1 teaspoon extract of peach. Sift flour several times and measure after sifting. Bake in shallow tins.
MRS. P. ELIZA PORTER.

CARAMEL SPONGE CAKE.

2 eggs beaten very light, 1 cup sugar, a little salt, 1/2 cup flour. Add these three ingredients a little at a time. 1/2 cup flour additional, 1 teaspoon baking powder, 1 teaspoon lemon extract, a small half cup of boiling water. Frosting:—1 cup sugar, 3 tablespoons water, boil until it hairs. Beat white of 1 egg stiff, stir into the frosting and spread on cake. Melt 1 square chocolate and spread on frosting.
ANNA M. GRAVES.

PLAIN CAKE.

1 egg, 1 cup sugar, 1 large teaspoon sour cream, 1 cup milk. Pinch of soda dissolved in milk, 2 cups flour, 2 teaspoons baking powder. Flavor with nutmeg and vanilla. Bake in shallow tin as layer cake.

MRS. D. W. WELLS.

SPONGE LAYER CAKE.

4 eggs, 1½ cups sugar, ½ cup cold water, 3 teaspoons baking powder, 3 small cups flour. Flavor with vanilla, makes 3 layers. Use any kind of cake filling.

MRS. A. H. GRAVES

COLD WATER SPONGE CAKE.

3 eggs beaten two minutes, 1½ cups sugar beaten into the eggs for five minutes, 1 cup of flour in which 2 teaspoons of baking powder have been mixed. Beat all together three minutes. ½ teacup of cold water beaten five minutes. A little salt, 1 more cup of flour. Beat all together three minutes.

MRS. CELIA E. WELLS.

LAYER CAKE.

1 cup of sugar, 1½ cups flour, ½ cup of milk, 2 eggs, 1 teaspoon cream tartar, ¼ teaspoon soda or 2 teaspoons baking powder. Bake in three layers and fill with 1 cup of whipped cream, or 1 lemon, grated rind and juice, 1 egg, 1 small cup of sugar, butter size of walnut. Beat all together and boil until thick. Spread between layers when cold.

MRS. R. M. WOODS.

ONE EGG CAKE.

1 egg, 1 cup sugar, ¾ cup milk, 1¾ cups flour, 3 teaspoons baking powder, 1 tablespoon butter. Flavor.

MRS. WIGHT.

SWISS CAKE.

2 eggs, 1 heaping cup of sugar, 1/4 cup of butter, 1 cup of sweet milk, 2½ cups of flour, 1½ teaspoons baking powder. Stir the butter and sugar to a cream. Beat the eggs thoroughly. This quantity makes two loaves.

MRS. L. S. BLISS.

ALBION CAKE.

1 cup sugar, ⅓ cup butter, ½ cup water, 2 eggs, (yolks,) 1⅓ cups flour, 3 even teaspoons baking powder. Cream the butter and sugar, then add the beaten yolks of the eggs, next the water, then flour, lastly whites of the eggs beaten very stiff.

MRS. A. AVERY.

CAKE FILLING.

1 cup cream, 1 cup sugar boiled twenty minutes, flavor to taste.

MRS. D. F. SHATTUCK.

WALNUT FILLING FOR CAKE.

Whites of 3 eggs beaten stiff, 3 large tablespoons white sugar, 1 cup chopped walnut meats, flavor to taste, or use boiled frosting into which stir the meats.

MRS. D. BILLINGS.

CHOCOLATE FILLING.

1 square of chocolate, 4 tablespoons of thick cream, ¾ of a cup of sugar, cook over steam.

MRS. ERNEST GODIN.

CREAM CHOCOLATE FILLING.

1 cup sweet cream, 1 cup sugar, 2 squares grated chocolate, 1 tablespoon flour. Cook as custard, letting the water boil twenty minutes. Beat until light.

MARION WARNER.

FILLING FOR LAYER CAKE.

Grate 1 large apple, add 1 cup sugar, stir for twenty minutes, add white of 1 egg beaten to a stiff froth, stir ten minutes, then add 1 teaspoon white rose and stir five minutes more.

MRS. B. M. WARNER.

CARAMEL CAKE.

3 eggs whites, 1 cup sugar, $\frac{1}{2}$ cup butter, $\frac{1}{2}$ cup milk, $1\frac{1}{2}$ cups flour, 1 heaping teaspoon baking powder. Flavor with vanilla.

CARAMEL FILLING.

Piece of butter size of an egg, 1 pint brown sugar, $\frac{1}{2}$ cup of milk. Boil twenty minutes or until quite thick. Pour over the cake while warm.

MARY K. BARNES.

LAYER CAKE.

$\frac{3}{4}$ cup sugar, $\frac{1}{2}$ cup milk, 1 heaping cup flour, 1 egg, little salt, 1 tablespoon melted butter, 2 teaspoons baking powder. Filling:—1 cup cream, 1 cup sugar, 1 square chocolate, grated, 1 dessert spoon flour. Boil twenty minutes. Scald cream, mix dry chocolate, sugar, flour and add to the cream, when cold beat with egg beater until thick enough to spread.

MRS. ALICE. L. BARDWELL.

SNOW CAKE.

1 cup pulverized sugar, $\frac{1}{2}$ cup butter, whites of 3 eggs beaten very light, $1\frac{1}{2}$ cups flour, $\frac{2}{3}$ cup sweet milk, scant 2 teaspoons baking powder, almond to flavor. To frost, beat 3 yolks to froth, 1 cup pulverized sugar. Flavor with vanilla.

MRS. J. E. PORTER.

COLD WATER CAKE.

2 cups sugar, 1 cup butter, 1 cup cold water, 4 cups flour, 2 eggs, 2 teaspoons cream tartar, 1 teaspoon soda. Nutmeg and fruit if you like. Makes 2 loaves.

PEARL CAKE.

¼ cup butter, 1 cup sugar, whites of 2 eggs, 1 cup milk, 2 full cups flour, 2 teaspoons baking powder, little salt, 1 teaspoon vanilla. Work butter and sugar thoroughly, then add milk, then flour with baking powder well mixed; lastly whites of eggs.
MRS. JAMES PORTER.

LAYER CAKE.

2 eggs, 1 cup sugar, 2 cups flour, ½ cup sweet milk, 1 teaspoon cream of tartar, ½ teaspoon of soda, 1 teaspoon of lemon extract Filling for cake:—2 cups sugar, 1 cup sweet cream. Boil together twenty minutes.
MRS. ERNEST GODIN.

WHITE FRUIT CAKE.

1 cup butter, 2 cups sugar, 1 cup milk, 3½ cups flour, 1 grated cocoanut, 1 pound citron, 1 pound almonds, blanched and cut fine, 2 heaping teaspoons baking powder, whites of 5 eggs. If dessicated cocoanut use 1 cup.
MRS. C. A. JONES.

LEMON CAKE.

1 pound flour, 1 pound sugar, ¾ pound butter, 7 eggs, juice of 1 lemon, rind of 2. The sugar, butter and yolks must be beaten a long time, adding by degrees the flour, whites last, 1 goblet currants, 1 teaspoon baking powder.
MRS. ELIHU MARSH.

ROLLED JELLY CAKE.

3 eggs, 1 cup sugar, 1 cup flour, 2 tablespoons cold water, pinch of salt, 1 heaping teaspoon baking powder. Beat yolks until light, then add sugar, water and salt, lastly stir in the flour and baking powder. Bake in a long tin well greased. Turn on a damp towel. Cover the top with jelly and roll.

MISS CLARA FOLEY.

ANOTHER.

2 eggs, 1 cup sugar, 1 cup flour, 1½ teaspoons baking powder, 3 tablespoons water. Bake in a dripping pan, spread with jelly. before cake is cold. Roll quickly.

MRS. D. W. WELLS.

QUEEN CAKE

¾ pound shortening, (½ pound butter, ¼ pound lard,) 1 pound sugar, 1 pound eggs, (9,) 1 cup milk, 5 cups flour, 2 teaspoons baking powder, ½ pound citron sliced thin and floured Will make two very large loaves, or three fair sized. If fruit is desired, take one pound of mixed raisins, currants and citron, leaving out the ½ pound citron in the above rule.

MRS. W. H. BELDEN.

SOUR MILK CAKE.

1 cup raisins, ½ cup butter, 1 cup sour milk, 1½ cups sugar, 3 cups flour, 1 teaspoon soda, 1 egg. Spice to suit the taste. Nutmeg, cloves, cinnamon.

MRS. C. E. HUBBARD.

SPICE CAKE.

1 cup sugar, 1 egg, ¾ cup of butter, 2½ cups flour, 1 cup buttermilk, 1 cup raisins, ½ cup molasses, 1 teaspoon soda 1 teaspoon cinnamon, 1 teaspoon cloves.

MRS. ERNEST GODIN.

CHOCOLATE MARBLE CAKE.

2 cups sugar, ½ cup butter, 1 cup milk, 3 cups flour, 2 eggs, 2 teaspoons baking powder, 2 squares chocolate. Dissolve chocolate in a little hot water. Add ½ cup sugar, 1 teaspoon vanilla. To this add three tablespoons of the mixture. 2 loaves.

MRS. G. MORTON.

LAYER CAKE.

3 eggs well beaten, 2 cups sugar, 2 cups flour, 2 large teaspoons baking powder. ½ cup cold water.

MRS. C. E. HUBBARD.

ANGEL CAKE.

5 eggs, whites only, ⅔ tumbler of sugar, ½ tumbler flour, ½ teaspoon vanilla, ½ cream tartar Beat the whites stiff. Add the sugar in which the vanilla and cream tartar has been mixed.

MRS. D. W. WELLS.

MARBLE CAKE.

1 egg, (or not,) 1 cup sugar, ½ cup each butter and sweet milk, 2 cups flour, 1 teaspoon baking powder, salt. For the dark part take a cup of the light batter. Add grated chocolate to make a dark brown. Put in alternate layers, the light on the top.

MRS. A. MATHEWS.

WHITE CAKE.

1 cup sugar, ½ cup butter, ⅔ cup milk, 2 cups flour, 2 teaspoons baking powder, 4 eggs, whites only.

MRS. R. S. ROSS.

FRUIT CAKE.

1 cup butter, 4 eggs, 1 cup sour milk, $3\frac{1}{2}$ cups flour, 2 cups raisins, $\frac{1}{2}$ cup citron, 2 cups currants, spices

MRS. R. S. ROSS.

WALNUT CAKE.

1 cup sugar, ¼ cup butter, ½ cup milk, $1\frac{1}{2}$ cups flour, 2 eggs beaten separately, 3 tablespoons baking power, 1 cup chopped walnuts.

MISS E. MORTON.

ANGEL CAKE.

4 eggs, whites only, well beaten, ¾ tumbler granulated sugar, ½ teaspoon cream tartar, ½ tumbler of flour, ½ teaspoon vanilla, salt. Bake in small round tins, with hole in center, about twenty minutes in moderate oven.

MRS. G. S. BELDEN.

DRIED APPLE FRUIT CAKE.

1 cup dried apples soaked over night, 1 cup molasses 1 cup salt pork chopped fine, 1 cup boiling water Pour the water over the pork, add the apples chopped fine, and the molasses. When cold add 2 eggs, $1\frac{1}{2}$ teaspoons of soda, 1 teaspoon cream tartar, 1 cups flour, all kinds spice. Chopped dates and fruit if you wish. Bake one hour in a stove oven.

MRS. R. B. ABBOTT.

NO EGG FRUIT CAKE.

1 cup of sugar, 1 cup molasses, 1 cup sour milk, ¾ cup butter, 1 rounded teaspoon soda, 1 teaspoon nutmeg, 1 teaspoon cinnamon, 1 teaspoon cloves, 1 cup seeded raisins, 1 cup currants, 4 cups flour Excellent and keeps well.

MRS. CELIA E. WELLS.

BLACK HILL CAKE

2 eggs, 1 cup sugar, ½ cup butter, ⅔ cup milk, ½ teaspoon soda, 1 teaspoon cream tartar, 2 cups flour Reserve ½ cup of the dough and put in it a tablespoon of molasses, yolk of an egg, ½ teaspoon each of cloves, cinnamon and nutmeg, put dark dough on top. Flavor the light part with lemon.

MRS. L. H. KINGSLEY.

BOILED FROSTING.

½ cup sugar boiled, white of 1 egg, ¼ teaspoon cream tartar, ¼ teaspoon corn starch, very light and fluffy.

MRS. C. W. MARSH.

ADDITION.

AUNT EMILY'S CAKE.

1 cup butter, 2 cups sugar, 3 eggs, 1 cup milk, 4 small cups flour, 1 teaspoon soda, 2 teaspoons cream tartar, (or 3 teaspoons baking powder.) Flavor.

CORRECTIONS.

Page 113.—Cake without eggs. Add 1 cup milk.

Page 117.—Plain Cake. Should read 1 large tablespoon of sour cream instead of teaspoon sour cream.

Page 123 —Fruit Cake. Add 1 teaspoon soda.

Page 123.—Dried Apple Fruit Cake. Should be slow oven, not stove oven.

Page 129.—Marshmallow Cookies. Add 1 teaspoon cream tartar, ½ teaspoon soda.

DOUGHNUTS, GINGER BREADS, COOKIES.

DOUGHNUTS. (VERY FINE.)

½ cup butter, 1 cup sugar, 1½ pints flour, 1½ teaspoons Royal Baking powder, 1 egg, 1½ cups milk. Put butter, sugar and egg together smooth. Sift flour and powder together, add it to the butter and milk etc Mix with a soft dough, flour well the board. Roll out dough to ¼ inch in thickness, cut out with large doughnut cutter, and fry in hot lard. Serve with sifted sugar over them. Makes 24 doughnuts.

DOUGHNUTS.

1 egg, ½ cup of sugar, piece of butter size of a butternut, 1 cup of milk, 2 teaspoons baking powder. Flour sufficient to roll out.

MRS. D. H. SHATTUCK.

DOUGHNUTS.

1 quart of flour, 1 cup sugar, 1 egg, 2 tablespoons shortening, 1 cup milk, 2 teaspoons baking powder, 1 small teaspoon salt. Nutmeg if you like.

MRS. D. P. MORTON.

DOUGHNUTS.

⅔ cup sugar, 1 cup milk, 1 egg, 1 teaspoon of cream tartar, ½ teaspoon soda, 1 large spoon shortening, little salt, flour sufficient to roll out. Roll in pulverized sugar, when taken from kettle.

MRS. R. B. ABBOTT.

GINGER WAFERS.

1 cup of molasses, 1 cup brown sugar, 1 cup of lard, ½ cup cold coffee, 2 even teaspoons soda, 1 of ginger, mix stiff. Roll thin and bake in quick oven.
MRS. C. D. BARDWELL.

CREAM GINGER BREAD.

2 cups flour, 1 cup molasses, ¾ cup sour cream, 1 teaspoon soda, 1 egg, 1 teaspoon ginger, 1 teaspoon cinnamon, ½ teaspoon salt.
MRS. J. S. WELLS.

GINGER SNAPS.

2 cups molasses, 1 cup sugar 1 cup shortning, 1 egg, 2 tablespoons soda, dissolve in little hot water, 2 teaspoons ginger, salt. Mix hard and roll very thin. Makes about 100.
MRS. G. S. BELDIN.

GINGER CAKE.

½ cup sugar, ½ cup molasses, ½ cup lard, salt, ½ cup sour milk, ¾ teaspoon soda, 1 teaspoon ginger. Spice if you like. Flour to drop from spoon.
MRS. O. S. GRAVES.

GINGER DROP CAKES.

½ cup butter, 1 cup sugar, 1 cup molasses, 1 cup water, 2 teaspoons soda, 1 teaspoon ginger, 1 teaspoon cinnamon, ¼ teaspoon cloves, currants, salt, 3½ cups flour.
MRS. A. L. BARDWELL.

OLIVE GINGER BREAD.

5½ cups flour, 2 cups molasses, 1 cup sour milk, or sweet, teaspoon of cream tartar, ½ cup butter, 2 teaspoons soda, 2 teaspoons ginger.
MISS EUNICE MORTON.

GINGER SNAPS.

1 cup molasses, 1/2 cup melted shortening, 1/2 teaspoon salt, 1/2 teaspoon ginger, small teaspoon soda. Flour enough to mix hard. Boil molasses five minutes. Take from stove and add lard, add other ingredients. Roll out thin and bake.

ANNA E. HARRIS.

COOKIES.

1 cup sugar, 1 egg, 1 cup sour cream, 2 cups flour, little nutmeg or caraway seed. Drop from spoon.

MRS. C. D. BARDWELL.

MARSHMALLOW COOKIES.

1 cup sugar, 1/2 cup butter, 2 eggs, 2 tablespoons milk, 2 1/2 cups flour. Cut in diamond shaped pieces, in the center place a marshmallow, fold the two opposite points, over the marshmallow and press together, after baked they will look like little baskets.

MRS. EDWARD ELDRIDGE.

SUGAR COOKIES.

2 cups sugar, 1/2 cup lard or butter, 1 egg, 1 cup sweet milk, 1 teaspoon lemon, 1 teaspoon soda, 2 teaspoons cream of tartar. Flour to roll.

MRS. ERNEST GODIN.

COOKIES.

1 cup molasses, 1/2 cup sugar, 1 egg, 1 teaspoon soda, 1 teaspoon salt. Let molasses come to a boil, beat in soda, cool a little, add the egg (beaten slightly,) sugar and salt and make very stiff with flour and roll thin.

MRS. C. E. WELLS.

SOUR CREAM COOKIES.

1 cup sugar, 2½ cups flour, ¾ cups sour cream, 1 teaspoon soda, a little salt, 1 egg Handle lightly and quickly, roll, then bake in quick oven.

MISS M. E. PHELPS.

TART CRUST.

3 cups flour, 1 cup lard, 1 teaspoon sugar, 3 teapoons water, 1 egg (white.) Rub flour and lard together, add sugar and egg well beaten, add water, roll about as thin as pie crust.

MRS E. B. DICKINSON.

LOVE KNOTS.

1 egg, 4 tablespoons sweet cream, 2 tablespoons sugar, pinch of salt. Flour to knead very hard, roll out, cut in narrow strips, tie each one in 2 or 3 knots and fry in hot lard, sprinkle with white sugar while hot.

ULA GRAVES.

COOKIES

3 cups sugar, 1 cup butter, 4 eggs, 4½ teaspoons baking powder, ¾ cup milk, flour enough to roll out. Makes large quantity.

MRS. A. H. GRAVES.

CRULLERS.

1 tablespoon butter, 5 tablespoons sugar, 4 eggs, little nutmeg. Mix very stiff and fry.

MRS. ELIHU MARSH.

CRULLERS.

3 eggs, 1 cup sugar, butter size of a butternut, little salt and nutmeg, flour to roll hard. Cut in squares, slash in narrow strips from one side nearly to the other, to look like fringe, fry in hot lard.

MRS. J. H. HOWARD.

CRULLERS.

1 egg, 2 tablespoons sugar, 2 tablespoons melted butter. Flour enough to make a stiff batter. Roll out the dough a quarter of an inch thick, cut in strips 2½ inches long and 1½ inches wide. Cut these into 6 small strips, leaving ¼ of an inch uncut at either end. Take up every other strip on fingers and pull apart, so that the uncut ends will nearly meet. Fry in hot fat.

MRS. I. B. LOWELL.

NUT CRACKERS.

1 pound English Walnuts, 3 eggs (whites,) 27 teaspoons pulverized sugar. Beat whites and sugar as for frosting. Chop the nuts fine and stir in. Spread this over saltines and bake twenty minutes in a slow oven.

LOUISA BARDWELL.

BRAMBLES.

Crust:—2 cups flour, 1 cup lard, whites of 2 eggs beaten stiff, 4 tablespoons water, ½ teaspoon soda, 1 teaspoon cream tartar, little salt. Filling:—1 cup chopped raisins, 1 cup sugar, 1 egg, 1 lemon (juice and rind.) Roll out crust and cut in small squares and put a teaspoon of filling in each. Draw the corners together and bake.

MRS. C. W. MARSH.

CRULLERS.

1 cup sugar, ½ cup shortening (butter,) 1 cup milk, 2 eggs, 2 teaspoons baking powder, nutmeg. Stir in flour to roll, cut in rings, set in the oven two or three minutes before frying.

MRS. G. A. BILLINGS.

PICKLES.

*"Turnpike road to people's hearts
I find, lies through their mouths, or
I mistake mankind"*

HIGDON PICKLES.

Take green tomatoes and chop fine. Salt them and let them stand twenty-four hours. 1 cup of salt to the gallon for the brine. Then pour off the water, and to every gallon of tomatoes add two quarts of chopped cabbage, 3 onions, 3 green peppers, (also chopped,) 3 pounds sugar, 2 quarts of vinegar, a desert spoon each of cinnamon, cloves, celery seed, and mustard seed. Heat the vinegar scalding hot, pour over, does not require cooking.

MRS. W. H. BELDEN.

PICCALILLI.

½ bushel green tomatoes, chopped fine, $1\frac{1}{2}$ pints vinegar, 4 green peppers, 3 tablespoons of salt, $2\frac{1}{2}$ cups brown sugar, 1 tablespoon each of cloves and all-spice. Boil until tender.

MRS. CHARLES BARTLETT.

SPICED CURRANTS.

3 pounds stemmed currants, 2 pounds brown sugar, ½ tablespoon each of ground cloves, all-spice and cinnamon, ½ pint vinegar. Boil to a jam.

MRS. A. H. GRAVES.

FRENCH CHOW CHOW.

For this chow chow, select 1 quart large green cucumbers, cut in small pieces, 1 quart tiny cucumbers, 2 inches long or less, 1 quart green tomatoes sliced or cut in bits, 1 large cauliflower divided into tiny flowerets, 4 large green peppers, cut in coarse bits. When ready put in a weak brine, a cup of salt to gallon of water. Soak pickle twenty-four hours. Scald in same brine and drain. Make paste of 6 tablespoons of ground mustard, 1 of tumeric, 1 cup flour, 1 cup sugar, 2 quarts vinegar. Mix the dry ingredients with a little of the vinegar, then add remainder of vinegar. Let this mixture scald, and stir until a smooth thick paste, then add pickles and it is done. If one like the flavor of onions, 6 small onions improve it. This chow chow is excellent the day after it is made, but better in a month of time. Put in jar.

MRS. W. H. BELDEN.

GRAPE CATSUP.

1 quart grapes, 1 quart brown sugar. Squeeze out the pulps and cover with vinegar. Boil pulps and vinegar and strain to remove the seeds, being careful not to let it burn, then add sugar and skins with 1 tablespoon each of cinnamon and all-spice and $\frac{1}{2}$ tablespoon cloves. Boil until the skins are tender.

MRS. WM. H. DICKINSON.

COLD CATSUP.

1 peck of ripe tomatoes peeled and chopped fine. Squeeze juice out, then add 1 tea cup onions chopped fine, 1 cup green peppers, 1 cup sugar, 1 pint vinegar, 2 stems grated horse radish, 1 ounce black mustard, 1 ounce white mustard, 1 ounce celery seed, salt to taste.

MISS CORNELIA BILLINGS.

SWEET PICKLED PEACHES.

10 pounds peaches, 7 pounds sugar, 1 quart vinegar, 1/2 ounce whole cloves, 1/2 ounce whole cinnamon.

MISS EMMA A. WAITE.

CHILI SAUCE.

18 ripe tomatoes, 2 peppers, 2 onions, 1 cup sugar, 2 1/2 cups vinegar, 2 teaspoons of salt, cloves and cinnamon. Boil one hour.

MRS. M. H. BURKE.

SWEET PICKLE (CITRON.)

7 pounds citron, 3 pounds sugar, 1 quart vinegar. All-spice, cinnamon and cloves. Cut citron in slices and let stand in salt and water over night. Drain, boil in water with a teaspoon of alum until soft. Boil sugar, spices and vinegar. Drain the citron and pour the syrup over it.

MISS LUCY COWLES.

MUSTARD PICKLE.

1 pint small onions, 1 quart cucumbers, 1 quart small green tomatoes, 1 head cauliflower, 3 green peppers. Boil tomatoes in water two or three minutes, not too much. Then pour over the whole, boiling salt and water. Let this stand over night, then pour over hot vinegar, and let stand two or three days, until pickled. Now take 1 pint of vinegar, 1 1/2 cups sugar, 1/2 cup flour, 2 tablespoons dry mustard. Mix the flour and mustard well, then wet with a little cold vinegar, heat vinegar and sugar together. When boiling put in flour and mustard, and stir until thickened then pour over the other. Four times this rule will make 2 gallons.

MRS. S. G. HUBBARD.

PICKLE LILLY.

1 peck green tomates, 3 onions, 3 large green peppers chopped fine. Place in a jar with alternate layers of salt. Let stand over night, in the morning drain, then cook in water until tender, drain again, add 1 quart vinegar, 1 cup sugar, 1 tablespoon each of cinnamon, all-spice and cloves.

MRS. WM. JONES.

PICCALILLI (without cooking.)

2 quart chopped tomatoes, 1 pint onions, ¼ pound peppers. Mix together with 1 teacup of salt, and let stand two days. Then drain and add ¼ pound white mustard seed and cover with cold vinegar. Put in stone jar.

MRS. A. H. GRAVES.

MUSK MELON PICKLE.

Take ripe melons, remove seeds and peel, cut in small pieces and put them into a small jar, cover with hot vinegar. Let them stand until next day, then pour off vinegar, heat and pour on again, repeat this process until the fourth day, then weigh the melons and to every 5 pounds, add 3 pounds of white sugar. 1 quart of vinegar and spice to taste. They should be whole spices and tied in a linen cloth, simmer until tender. Take out fruit and boil the syrup until there is just enough to cover pickles.

MRS. H. L. WILLIAMS.

CUCUMBER PICKLES.

1 quart of rock salt, 1 gallon vinegar 2 gallons water scalded to dissolve the salt. Cool, and throw in cucumbers as they are picked. When wanted for use put into spiced vinegar. They will keep a long time in this preparation.

ONION PICKLE.

The white onions called silver skin are the best for pickling. They should be of uniform size, as large as a hickory nut. Pour boiling water on them, and the peeling can be quickly done. Drop the peeled onions in cold salt water. Let them stand over night. The next day, take out of the water and drain. Then put them in jars with mustard seed, whole mace and whole peppers. Pour on strong cold vinegar until the onions are covered. The jar should be closely covered and set away. They are ready for use in two days.

MRS. R. M. WOODS.

PRESERVES AND JELLIES.

"In everything you do aim to excel
For what is worth doing, is worth doing well"

PREPARING FRUIT FOR PRESERVING.

Blackberries,	Boil moderately about Six			minutes.
Plums,	"	"	" Ten	"
Raspberries,	"	"	" Six	"
Cherries,	"	"	" Five	"
Strawberries,	"	"	" Eight	"
Whortleberries,	"	"	" Five	"
Bartlett Pears (halves,)	"	"	" Twenty	"
Small sour Pears (whole)	"	"	" Thirty	"
Peaches halves.	"	"	" Eight	"
Peaches whole,	"	"	" Fifteen	"
Sour Apples (quartered)	"	"	" Ten	"
Ripe Currants,	"	"	" Six	"
Wild Grapes,	"	"	" Ten	"
Tomatoes,	"	"	" Sixty	"

AMOUNT OF SUGAR TO A QUART JAR.

Cherries,	Six ounces.
Strawberries,	Eight "
Raspberries,	Four "
Blackberries,	Six "
Quince,	Ten "
Sour Pears,	Eight "
Wild Grapes,	Eight "
Peaches,	Four "
Bartlett Pears,	Six "
Pine Apple,	Six "
Plums,	Eight "
Pie Plant,	Ten "
Ripe Currants,	Eight "
Cranberries,	Twelve "
Sour Apples (quartered,)	Six "

ORANGE MARMALADE.

12 medium sized oranges, slice them leaving out end piece and seeds. With water added make 7 pints. Let stand twenty-four hours. Boil until tender, then add 1 pound sugar to 1 pint fruit and the juice of 2 lemons. Boil ten or fifteen minutes and put in cans or jelly tumblers.

GOOSEBERRY JAM.

Top and stem the berries and wash them clean. Drain and weigh them. Take equal quantities of berries and white sugar. Stir them well together. Put them in a preserving kettle and boil for an hour, stirring them constantly to keep them from burning. When soft, mash. Put in jelly tumblers and when cold cover as for any jelly. Serve with cold meats.

MRS. DAVID BILLINGS.

CURRANT JELLY.

Wash the currants clean, drain, put in a bag and mash them. Squeeze out all the juice. To every pint of juice allow 1 pound sugar, put the juice in a kettle over the fire and heat; add the sugar and let come to a boil, stirring and skimming as required. Boil from ten to twelve minutes. Pour into tumblers.

MRS. R. BILLINGS.

BLACKBERRY PRESERVE.

7 pounds fruit, 3½ pounds sugar, 1 pint good vinegar; scald together and let stand twenty-four hours. Then pour off juice and scald it, and let it stand another twenty-four hours. Then scald all together, and put in cans. This will keep a year or more.

MISS A. P. LYMAN.

LEMON JELLY.

1 box gelatine, 1 pint cold water, let it stand one-half hour to one hour. Add 1 quart boiling water, 1½ pints sugar, the juice of 5 and grated rind of 2 lemons. Strain into jelly mould and set in cool place.

MRS. S. G. HUBBARD.

LEMON JELLY.

Soak 1 box of gelatine in 1 cup of cold water. Add 1 quart boiling water, 2 cups sugar and 1 cup lemon juice, strain into a mould and let it harden.

MISS MARIA L. PORTER.

QUINCE HONEY.

1 quart sugar, 1 pint water, 2 teacups grated quince. Boil fifteen minutes and pour into jelly tumblers.

M. L. PORTER.

GREEN GRAPE MARMALADE.

Pick the grapes from stems, wash and put in a porcelain kettle with a small bowl of water, boil slowly until soft enough for the seeds to slip out, then strain, to 1 bowl of grape juice add 1 bowl of granulated sugar, cook slowly half an hour or until thick enough to cut with a knife when cool.

CORNELIA A. BILLINGS.

TO PRESERVE BLACKBERRIES.

7 pounds of berries and $3\frac{1}{2}$ pounds of sugar, 1 pint of good vinegar, scald all together and let it stand twenty-four hours, then turn off the juice and scald it and let it stand twenty-four hours and then scald all together.

A. LYMAN.

BUTTERCUP JELLY.

$\frac{1}{2}$ package gelatine soaked in $\frac{1}{2}$ cup cold water two hours, 3 eggs, 1 pint of milk, 1 heaping cup sugar, 1 teaspoon vanilla, bit of soda size of a pea stirred into milk. Scald milk, stir in soaked gelatine until that is dissolved and strain through coarse cloth. Add sugar and yolks of eggs, return to kettle and stir until it begins to thicken. Let cool and add flavoring, whip white of 1 egg stiff. When yellow jelly coagulates around edges, beat it with the white of egg.

MRS. DAVID BILLINGS.

CIDER JELLY.

1 box gelatine, 1 pint water to dissolve. Let stand twenty minutes, add 1 pint boiling water, $1\frac{1}{2}$ pints cider, $1\frac{1}{4}$ pounds sugar, juice and rind of 1 lemon. Let it boil with the mixture. Let it stand in pan of cold water until quite cool. Strain through flannel.

MISS MARY BRIGGS.

CIDER APPLE SAUCE

3 pails sweet apples, 3 quarts boiled cider, 1 pint molasses, 1 peck quinces. Boil 4 hours slowly.

MRS. J. H. SANDERSON.

ORANGE JELLY.

1 box gelatine soaked in 2 cups cold water, $2\frac{1}{2}$ cups sugar, juice of 4 oranges and grated rind of 2, 3 cups of boiling water. Soak gelatine two hours, add juice, and grated rind and sugar and leave for 1 hour. Pour in boiling water. Stir until dissolved; strain through double flannel

MRS. DAVID BILLINGS.

PRESERVED PEARS.

8 pounds of pears, 4 pounds of sugar, $\frac{1}{4}$ pound of ginger root, 3 lemons, $1\frac{1}{2}$ pints of water. Slice the pears very thin, also the lemon very thin. Prepare the syrup with water, sugar and ginger root. When heated to boiling put in pears and lemons, boil until pears are very tender, almost clear, then skim out pears, ginger root and lemons, boil down the syrup quite thick and pour over the whole.

MRS. SAMUEL BILLINGS.

CURRANT CONSERVE.

5 pounds currants, 5 pounds sugar, 2 pounds raisins, 4 oranges, squeeze juice of oranges on sugar put the peel of 3 in cold water and let come to a boil slowly to remove bitter taste. Chop rather fine, stone the raisins and chop, add to currants, sugar and oranges and boil slowly twenty minutes, put into jelly tumblers.

MRS. E. L. DICKINSON.

BEVERAGES.

"Drink, pretty creature, drink."—Wordsworth.

BEEF TEA.

1 pound lean beef cut into small pieces. Put into a jar without a drop of water, cover tightly and set in a dish of cold water. Heat gradually to a boil and continue this for three or four hours, until the meat is white. Season with salt; when cold skim.

MRS. G. A. BILLINGS.

BEEF EXTRACT.

Take lean beef, chop in fine pieces, place in glass fruit jar, sprinkle on just a little salt and seal tightly. Place in a kettle of water and boil four hours. Remove bits of meat before using.

MRS. E. A. HUBBARD.

RASPBERRY VINEGAR.

2 quarts raspberries, 1 pint vinegar. Let stand three or four days, mash and strain through a bag. Add 1 pound sugar to each pint juice. Boil twenty minutes, skim; bottle when cold.

RED RASPBERRY SHRUB.

3 pints raspberries, 1 pint vinegar. Let stand three or four days, strain. To every pint of juice add 1 pound of sugar. Boil twenty minutes. Bottle when cold.

CURRANT SHRUB.

To 1 pint currant juice add 1 pound loaf sugar. Boil five minutes, stir it constantly while cooking, and when cold bottle it. 1 or 2 spoonfuls in a tumbler of water affords a refreshing beverage.

LEMON SYRUP.

1 pound loaf sugar to 1 pint lemon juice. Let it stand twenty-four hours or until sugar is dissolved, stirring it often. When dissolved wring a flannel bag very dry in hot water and strain the syrup. Bottle. This will keep a long time.

BLACKBERRY CORDIAL.

1 quart juice, $\frac{1}{2}$ pound loaf sugar, $\frac{1}{4}$ ounce nutmeg, $\frac{1}{4}$ ounce ground cinnamon, $\frac{1}{8}$ ounce ground all-spice. Boil five or six minutes. When cool add 1 pint best brandy. For sickness.

MRS. M. L. PEASE.

MEAD.

3 pounds white sugar. Pour over it 3 pints of boiling water, 1 pint of molasses, $\frac{1}{4}$ pound tartaric acid, 1 ounce sassafras. Bottle and use as a syrup with soda.

INDIAN MEAL GRUEL.

1 tablespoon Indian or oat meal, a pinch of salt. Mix the meal smooth with cold water. Pour upon this a pint of boiling water, and turn into a sauce pan to boil gently one-half an hour. Stir frequently. Strain and add a tablespoon of cream. Some persons like it sweetened and a little nutmeg added, but to many it is more palatable without either.

MILK PORRIDGE.

2 cups oat meal, 2 cups water, 2 cups milk. Soak the oat meal over night in the water. Strain in the morning, and boil the water half an hour. Put in the milk. Salt to taste. Boil up once and serve.

SODA CREAM.

Mix together in a sauce pan, 1 pound sugar, 1 egg, 1 tablespoon of flour, 1 pint cold water, juice of 1 lemon. Put over the fire and let scald, remove and add 1 ounce of tartaric acid and 1 tablespoon of flavoring. This will make 1 quart of syrup. Bottle and keep on ice, when ready for use put 2 tablespoons of cream in glass, fill half full of cold water and add $\frac{1}{4}$ teaspoon baking soda.

MRS. O. S. GRAVES.

TO MAKE COFFEE.

1 tablespoon coffee for each person. Mix it with an egg and cold water to make a paste; then add boiling water and boil five or ten minutes. Settle the coffee with a little cold water. Serve with cream or hot milk.

TO MAKE COFFEE BY FILTERING.

Put coffee in the strainer and pour over it boiling water. If not strong enough, let it drip again.

TO MAKE TEA.

Scald tea-pot. 1 teaspoon of tea for 1 cup. Pour over boiling water and let stand on back of stove five minutes.

CHOCOLATE.

1 quart water, 1½ pints milk, 2 squares Baker's chocolate. Sweeten to taste. Steam in a double boiler two hours.

MRS. C. A. JONES.

CONFECTIONERY.

"Sweet to the sweet"—Shakespeare.

FRENCH VANILLA CREAM.

Break into a bowl the white of 1 or more eggs, and add to it an equal quantity of cold water. Then stir in confectioner's sugar until you have it stiff enough to mould into shape with the fingers. Flavor to taste. This can be used for plain creams or English walnuts. Dates or any kind of nuts or fruit can be added. Grated maple sugar or chocolate added to the cream makes a nice confection.

ORANGE DROPS.

Grate the rind of 1 orange and squeeze the juice over it. Strain, then stir in confectioner's sugar until it is stiff enough to form into small balls. Cocoanut grated can be added to above.

FUDGE.

2 cups granulated sugar, 1 cup cream, $\frac{1}{4}$ cake of Baker's chocolate, a piece of butter ($\frac{1}{2}$ the size of an egg,) 1 teaspoon of vanilla. Cut the chocolate up, put it with sugar, cream and butter in a sauce pan. Boil until it forms a soft ball in cold water. Remove from the fire, add the vanilla and stir until it will just spread on buttered tins.

MABEL BILLINGS.

FUDGE.

2 cups sugar, ½ cup milk, 1 square of chocolate. Heat the milk, grate chocolate and mix dry with sugar, then pour the heated milk over it with the butter. Cook and when it grains by stirring a little in a saucer pour in a cup of either cocoanut or chopped nuts and 2 teaspoons of vanilla. Remove from the stove and beat well. Pour into a buttered tin and when nearly cold cut into squares.

HELEN SMITH.

PEANUT TAFFY.

1 pint molasses, ½ cup sugar, 1 tablespoon vinegar, a piece of butter the size of an egg. Boil until it is brittle in water, add a pinch of soda. Put in the meats of a quart of peanuts and pour on buttered pans.

MABEL BILLINGS.

WALNUT CREAM.

2 cups of coffee A sugar, 1 cup cream, 1 quart hickory nuts or 1 pound of English walnuts. Boil the sugar and cream until it becomes brittle in cold water. Put in the meats, stirring well, and set away on buttered plates to harden. Be sure that it is boiled enough else it will not harden.

SALTED PEANUTS.

Buy the raw peanuts and shell. Pour boiling water on them and let stand a few minutes until the skins slip off easily. Melt a little butter in a dripping pan, put in the prepared peanuts, sprinkle them with a little salt, then place on the grate in a moderate oven. Turn occasionally until browned as much as desired.

MRS. CHARLES L. GRAVES.

GLACI NUTS.

2 cups sugar, just enough water to dissolve the sugar. Boil to the "crackle" and drop in English walnuts, Brazil nuts; bits of orange, pineapple or any fruit you prefer. Remove at once and place on buttered plates and cool immediately.

BUTTER SCOTCH.

1 cup sugar, $\frac{1}{2}$ cup cold water, $\frac{1}{2}$ cup vinegar, butter size of butternut, pour in buttered pan.

MRS. SETH KINGSLEY.

FUDGE.

2 cups sugar, 1 cup milk, 2 squares chocolate. Butter size of a small egg. Boil all together until it hairs. Remove from stove and stir until it grains. Pour into buttered tins until it hardens.

MRS. R. BILLINGS.

CREAM TAFFY.

1 cup granulated sugar, 1 tablespoon vinegar, $\frac{1}{2}$ cup water. Let ingredients boil until the candy will crack when dropped in water. Pour into buttered pans to cool, then flour the hands and pull the taffy until white.

ULA GRAVES.

FRENCH CREAM CANDY COOKED.

4 cups white sugar, 1 cup hot water, flavor with vanilla. Put the sugar and water in a pan and let it boil without stirring, about eight minutes. If creamy, and will roll in a ball between the fingers, pour the whole into a bowl and beat rapidly. If not boiled enough to cream, cook a little longer, but not too much. Add the flavoring. This is the foundation for all French creams. It can be used in any shape.

MARGERY DAW.

MOLASSES CANDY.

2 cups molasses, 1 cup sugar, 1 tablespoon butter, 1 tablespoon vinegar, 1 teaspoon soda.

MRS. EUROTAS MORTON.

CHOCOLATE CARAMELS.

1 cup rich sweet cream, 1 cup brown sugar, 1 cup white sugar, 7 tablespoons grated chocolate, 1 tablespoon corn starch stirred into the cream also soda the size of a pea. 1 tablespoon butter. Boil all these ingredients together except the chocolate and ½ of the cream, stirring often to keep from burning. Boil half hour. Mix chocolate with cream adding little water if necessary. Draw the sauce pan to the back of the stove and stir well while adding the chocolate and cream, then let all cook together for fifteen minutes or until it makes a hard glossy coat on the spoon. Pour into buttered tins and cut into squares.

MRS. GEO. BARNES.

MOLASSES TAFFY.

½ cup molasses, 1 cup white sugar, 1 tablespoon vinegar, 2 cups water. Butter size of an egg.

MRS. GEO. BELDEN.

PEANUT CANDY.

1 cup sugar melted, ⅔ cup chopped nuts. When sugar is melted stir in the nuts and pour on a sheet of tin.

EUNICE MORTON.

PANOCHEE CANDY.

4 cups brown sugar, 1 cup of milk, butter size of a walnut. Cook about twenty minutes then put in a tablespoon of vanilla and the meats of 1 pound of English walnuts. Spread on a buttered dish.

MISS HELEN SMITH.

SALTED ALMONDS.

Shell 1 pound almonds. Pour on boiling water and let stand until the red skins will slip off easily. Place the nuts on a tin and rub them with a piece of butter the size of a walnuts. Shake salt over all, do not get them too salt. Set them in a moderate oven and let brown as much as desired.

MRS. GEO. BARNES.

COCOANUT CAKES.

2 cups sugar, $\frac{1}{2}$ cup water. Boil until it crisps in water, take off the fire and stir until it creames, after the candy is beaten to a cream, stir in 1 grated cocoanut, make in good sized cakes but thin. Different kinds of nuts can be used or fruit if desired.

NUT CANDY.

1 cup milk or cream, 4 cups brown sugar, 1 cup of nuts. Butter size of an egg, a desert spoon of vanilla. When done, make into squares.

MARION WARNER.

PEPPERMINTS.

2 cups sugar, $\frac{1}{2}$ cup water. Boil five minutes, flavor with peppermint, stir till thick and creamy, drop on buttered paper.

MRS. I. B. LOWELL.

MISCELLANEOUS.

"Variety is the spice of life which gives all its flavor."

TO EXTERMINATE RED ANTS.

Tie sulphur in a cotton cloth and place where they are troublesome. Small piece of camphor gum or elder leaves will sometimes drive them away.

SODA.

Common baking soda is excellent for scalds and burns. Moisten the burned place and sprinkle on the soda. It seems to withdraw the heat and with it the pain.

REMEDY FOR COUGH.

Take the juice of 1 lemon, 1 dessert spoon vaseline, ½ cup sugar and the white of one egg. Beat all together. Take spoonful every hour.

MRS. A. WARNER.

LAXATIVE FIG CONSERVE.

½ pound of figs, chopped fine, 1 ounce of powdered senna leaves, 1 dram cardamom seeds, (pulverized,) ½ pint molasses. Let molasses come to a boil add chopped figs and other ingredients, keep in jelly tumblers. Dose, ½ teaspoon just before retiring.

MRS. R. M. WOODS.

HAM BRINE.

To 1 pail of water 2 quarts salt, 1 tablespoon saltpetre, 1 tablespoon of ammonia, 1 tablespoon baking soda, 1 teacup of molasses, 1 teacup of sugar. Stir all together till dissolved, add this cold.

MRS. DWIGHT MORTON.

SAUSAGE.

30 pounds meat, 12 ounces fine salt, 2½ ounces pepper 2 cups sage, 1½ cups savory if desired.

MRS. A. PECK.

PICKLE FOR HAM.

For 1 hundred pounds of pork, allow 6 pounds salt, 2 pound light brown sugar, 2 ounces saltpetre. Water sufficient to cover hams. Boil and skim until clear. Just before taking from fire add 1 ounce soda. When cold pour this pickle over the ham.

MRS E. B. DICKINSON.

SAND BAG FOR THE SICK ROOM.

Get some clear, fine sand, dry it thoroughly in a kettle on the stove, make a bag about eight inches square of flannel, fill it with the sand, sew the opening carefully together and cover the bag with cotton or linen.

JAPANESE CLEANSING FLUID.

2 ounces spirits of ammonia, 1 ounce ether, 1 ounce alcohol, 1 ounce glycerine. All put in 1 bottle at druggists, 2 ounces white powdered castile soap, put up in white paper. Dissolve soap in 1 pint of water over the fire, add 2 quarts of boiling water, when nearly cold add the bottle of ingredients. Will keep for years in bottles when securely corked.

MRS. R. M. WOODS.

WASHING FLUID.

1 pound Babbit's Potash, 1 ounce dry ammonia, 1 ounce salts tartar, 1 ounce borax, 4 quarts hot water. Dissolve potash in the hot water and when a little cool add the other ingredients. Soak the clothes in warm water over night. In the morning put into boiler of cold water to which has been added, ⅔ cup of fluid and ⅓ bar of soap. Boil fifteen minutes. Put through 2 tubs water and hang up to dry.

MRS. J. E. PORTER.

POULTICE FOR SORE THROAT.

2 tablespoons Indian Meal, 2 tablespoons wood ashes, 1 tablespoon mustard, 1 tablespoon salt. Mix with hot water to a thick dough, put in a woolen stocking and bind on the neck at night.

MRS. W. H. BELDEN.

GLOSS STARCH.

To give high gloss to shirts, collars and cuffs, add a little dissolved gum arabic to the starch. A bottle of this should be kept in the laundry. Prepare by pouring an ounce of boiling water over 2 ounces of white gum arabic, add a teaspoon powdered borax and bottle before it gets quite cold. 1 tablespoon of this added to a quart of starch gives a nice gloss.

MRS. GEO. BARNES.

"Hot sunshine will remove scorch."

"Clothes dry much quicker when borax is added to the hot starch just before using."

"To remove soot from carpet, cover thickly with salt and then brush up."

"When a felon first begins to make its appearance, take a lemon, cut off one end, insert the finger, and change every three hours."

"To remove paint or grease spots, take four tablespoons alcohol and one of salt, shake well together and apply with a sponge or brush."

INDEX.

	PAGE
SOUPS.	
Tomato Soup, No. 1,	5
" " No. 2,	5
Tomato Bisque,	5
Vegetable Soup,	6
Potato Soup, No. 1,	6
Chicken Soup, No. 1,	6
Mock Turtle Soup,	6
Chicken Soup, No. 2,	7
Cabbage Soup, No. 1,	7
" " No. 2,	7
Pea Soup,	7
Clam Soup,	7
Potato Soup, No. 2,	8
Turkey Soup,	8
Clam Chowder,	8
Bean Soup,	8
Celery Soup,	9
Black Bean Soup, (fine,)	9
Ham and Egg Soup,	9
Asparagus Soup,	10
Milk Soup,	10
Turnip and potato Soup,	10
Parsnip Stew,	10
Lamb Soup,	11
Soup Stock,	11
FISH.	
Baked Fish, (a la creme,)	15
Hollandaise Sauce for Fish,	15
Broiled Oysters,	16
Oyster Fritters,	16

	PAGE
To Fry Oysters,	16
Rhode Island Fish Cakes,	16
Escalloped Fish,	16
Fried Salt Cod Fish,	17
Escalloped Oysters, No. 1,	17
Baked Fish,	17
Escalloped Salmon,	17
Escalloped Oysters, No. 2,	17
Fish Croquettes,	17
MEATS.	
Roast Turkey, Chicken or Duck,	21
Roast Veal,	21
Spiced Veal,	21
Veal Cutlets,	22
To Warm-Over Meat,	22
Scalloped Chicken,	22
Roast Pork,	23
Roast Lamb,	23
Lamb Stewed with Peas,	23
Frizzled Beef,	23
Broiled Beefsteak,	23
Grilled Chicken,	24
Mutton Pie Plain,	24
Chicken Pie,	24
Pot Roast,	24
Mock Duck,	25
Escalloped Meat, No. 1,	25
" " No. 2,	25
Stuffed Beef,	25
Beef a la Mode,	26
Potted Ham,	26

	PAGE
Pressed Chicken,	26
Veal Pattie,	27
Round Steak,	27
Fried Tripe,	27
Mutton Pie with Tomatoes,	27
Meat Pie,	27
Ragout of Meat,	27
Beefsteak Smothered in Onions	28
Beefsteak Omelet,	28
Veal Loaf, (excellent,)	28
Beef Loaf,	28

GRAVIES AND SAUCES FOR MEATS.

Giblet Sauce,	33
Brown Gravy Sauce,	33
Oyster Sauce,	33
Mint Sauce,	33
Caper Sauce for Leg of Lamb,	33
Gravy for Boiled or Baked Fish,	34
Bread Sauce,	34
Tomato Sauce,	34
Tartare Sauce,	34

VEGETABLES.

Vegetables, preparing-cooking,	37
Potato Souffle,	38
Stuffed and Baked Tomatoes,	38
To Boil Cauliflower,	38
Stuffed Potatoes,	38
Boiled Dinner,	39
Boiling Vegetables,	39
Potato Balls,	39
Fried Parsnips,	39
A nice way to cook Cabbage,	40
Stewed Cabbage,	40
Tremont Potatoes,	40
Baked Rice and Tomatoes,	40
Beat Hash,	41
Parsnips Fritters,	41
Macaroni Boiled,	41
Macaroni in Cream,	41
An old-fashioned Dish,	41
Baked Beans,	42

BREAKFAST AND TEA DISHES.

	PAGE
Duchess Potatoes,	47
Escalloped Potatoes, No. 1,	47
Potato cakes,	47
Risotto Napolitaine,	48
Graham Griddle Cakes,	48
Potato Croquettes,	48
Sweet Breads on Toast,	49
Croquettes,	49
Rice Omelet,	49
Veal Pattee,	49
Rice Croquettes,	50
Chicken Croquettes, No. 1,	50
" " No. 2,	50
Chicken Souffle,	51
Escalloped Potatoes, No. 2,	51
Cream Potatoes,	51
Smothered Sausage,	51
Pressed Chicken,	52
Beaf Loaf,	52
Veal Loaf,	52
Apple Fritters,	52
Snowy Omelet,	52
Beef Steak Omelet,	53
Meat Omelet,	53
Ragout of Meat,	53
Omelet,	53
Pressed Eggs,	53
Egg Omelet,	53
Welsh Rare Bit,	54
Corn Fritters,	54
Corn Oysters,	54
Ham and Egg on Toast,	54
Baked Omelet,	54
Baked Eggs,	55
Waffles, No. 1,	55
" No. 2,	55

SALADS.

Chicken or Veal Salad,	59
Salad Dressing, No. 1,	59
" " No. 2,	59
" " No. 3,	60
Cabbage Salad, No. 1,	60
" " No. 2,	60

INDEX—HATFIELD COOK BOOK.

	PAGE		PAGE
Cream Salad,	60	Parker House Rolls, No. 1,	71
Boiled Dressing,	61	Breakfast Muffins,	72
Salad Dressing, No. 4,	61	Buns,	72
" " No. 5	61	Muffins,	72
Lobster Salad,	61	Parker House Rolls, No. 2,	72
Potato Salad, No. 1,	62	Baking Powder Biscuit,	72
" " No. 2,	62	Rolls,	73
Salad Dressing, No. 5,	62	Top Overs,	73
Veal Salad,	62	Wheat Gems,	73
		Parker House Rolls, No. 3,	73
WEIGHTS AND MEASURES.		Pop Overs or Breakfast Cakes,	74
Remarks	64	Breakfast Pocket Books,	74
		Pan Cakes,	74
BREADS.		Pop Overs,	74
Potato Yeast, No. 1,	65	Sally Lunn,	74
" " No. 2,	65	Green Corn Griddle Cakes,	75
Wheat Bread, No. 1,	65	Corn Fritters,	75
Bread Twice Raised,	66	Good Corn Bread,	75
Wheat Bread, No. 2,	66		
Graham Bread, No. 1,	66		
" " No. 2,	66	PUDDINGS AND SAUCES.	
" " No. 3,	66	Tirebot Cream Pudding,	77
Graham Crackers,	67	Baked Apple Dumpling,	77
Graham Bread, No. 4,	67	Baked Suet Pudding,	78
" " No. 5,	67	Snow Pudding,	78
Oat Meal Bread,	67	Cream Tapioca,	78
Graham Rolls,	67	Baked Indian Pudding,	79
Baked Brown Bread,	68	Delicate Indian Pudding,	79
Steamed Brown Bread, No. 1,	68	Chocolate Pudding, No. 1,	79
Brown Bread, No. 1,	68	Graham Pudding,	79
" " No. 2,	68	Chocolate Pudding, No. 2,	80
Steamed Brown Bread, No. 2,	68	Corn Starch Pudding,	80
Brown Bread, No. 3,	69	Judge Peter's Pudding,	80
Indian Meal Rolls,	69	Bread Pudding,	80
Raised Biscuit, No. 1,	69	Rice Pudding,	81
Gems,	69	Prune Pudding, No. 1,	81
Raised Biscuit, No. 2,	69	" " No. 2,	81
Rye Muffins,	70	Huckleberry Pudding,	81
Johnny Cake, No. 1,	70	Quaking Pudding,	82
" " No. 2,	70	Steam Pudding,	82
Raised Griddle Cakes,	70	Cottage Pudding,	83
Wheat Rolls,	70	Kingsley Pudding,	83
Newport Rolls,	71	Graham Pudding,	83
German Sponge,	71	Sweet Corn Pudding,	83
French Rolls,	71	Berry Pudding,	83
Wheat Muffins,	71	Custard Souffle Pudding,	84

	PAGE
Apple Pudding,	84
Caramel Pudding,	84
Orange Pudding, No. 1,	85
" " No. 2,	85
Pineapple Pudding,	85
Indian Pudding,	85
English Plum Pudding,	86
Suet Pudding,	86
Imperial Rice Pudding,	86
Creme, diplomate,	87
Cracker Pudding,	87
Pudding Sauces, No. 1,	87
" " No. 2,	87
" " No. 3,	87
" " No. 4,	88
Rice Pudding,	88

PIES.

Pie Crust,	91
Puff Paste, (very nice,)	91
Nice Mince Pie,	91
Mince Meat for Pies,	92
Strawberry Cream Pie,	92
Cream Pie, No. 1,	92
" " No. 2,	92
" " No. 3,	93
Squash Pie, No. 1,	93
Cranberry Pie,	93
Lemon Meringue Pie,	93
Rhubarb Pie,	93
Lemon Pie, No. 1,	94
Mock Mince Pie,	94
Squash Pie, No. 2,	94
Cream Pie, No. 4,	94
Custard Pie,	94
Chocolate Pie,	94
Cocoanut Pie,	95
Chicken Pie,	95
Apple Pudding Pies,	95
Rice Pie,	95
Lemon Pie, No. 2,	95

PLAIN and FANCY DESSERTS.

Pine Apple Cream,	99
Whipped Apple Cream,	99
Coffee Blanc Mange,	99

	PAGE
Tapioca Cream,	100
Prune Whip,	100
Cheese Straws, No. 1,	100
" " No. 2,	101
Short Cake,	101
Strawberry Short Cake,	101
Raspberry Tapioca,	101
Chocolate Blanc Mange,	102
Orange Custard,	102
Baked Custard,	102
Boiled Custard,	102
Coffee Puff, No. 1,	103
" " No. 2,	103
Coffee Jelly,	103
Pineapple Ice,	103
Milk Sherbet, No. 1,	103
Beaten Cream,	103
Milk Sherbet, No. 2,	104
Ice Cream, No. 1,	104
Raspberry Puff,	104
Coffee Ice Cream,	104
Caramel Ice Cream,	104
Vanilla Ice Cream,	105
Strawberry Sherbet,	105
Ice Cream, No. 2,	105
Lemon Ice, No. 1,	105
Lemon Ice, No. 2,	106
Ice Cream, No. 3,	106
Nut Ice Cream,	106

CAKES.

Macaroons,	109
Cocoanut Cake, No. 1,	109
Pop Doodle,	109
Hermit Cake,	110
Pound Cake,	110
Filling for Cake,	110
Black Fruit Cake,	110
Black or Wedding Cake,	110
Walnut Cake, No. 1,	111
Chocolate Cake, No. 1,	111
Sponge Cake, No. 1,	111
Angel Cake, No. 1,	111
Orange Cake,	112
Quick Loaf Cake,	112

INDEX—HATFIELD COOK BOOK.

	PAGE		PAGE
Sunshine Cake,	112	Sour Milk Cake,	121
Cream Puffs,	112	Spice Cake,	122
Pork Cake,	113	Chocolate Marble Cake,	122
Chocolate Cake, (devil's food,)	113	Layer Cake, No. 3,	122
Halligar Cake,	113	Angel Cake, No. 1,	122
Cake without Eggs,	113	Marble Cake,	122
Cocoanut Cake, No. 2,	113	White Cake,	122
Coffee, Cake,	114	Fruit Cake, No. 2,	123
Fig Cake,	114	Walnut Cake, No. 2,	123
Composition Cake,	114	Angel Cake, No. 2,	123
Chocolate Cake, No. 2,	114	Dried Apple Fruit Cake,	123
Cream Sponge Cake,	114	No Egg Fruit Cake,	123
Fruit Cake,	115	Black Hill Cake,	124
Raised Cake, No. 1,	115	Boiled Frosting.	124
" " No. 2,	115	DOUGHNUTS, GINGER BREADS, COOKIES.	
Raised Dough Cake,	115		
Sponge Cake,	115	Doughnuts, (very fine,)	127
Raised Loaf Cake,	116	Doughnuts, No. 1,	127
Lemon Cake, No. 1,	116	Doughnuts, No. 2,	127
Delicate Cake,	116	Doughnuts, No. 3,	127
Caramel Sponge Cake,	116	Ginger Wafers,	128
Plain Cake,	117	Cream Ginger Bread,	128
Sponge Layer Cake,	117	Ginger Snaps, No. 1,	128
Cold Water Sponge Cake,	117	Ginger Cake,	128
Layer Cake, No. 1,	117	Ginger Drop Cakes,	128
One Egg Cake,	117	Olive Ginger Bread,	128
Swiss Cake,	118	Ginger Snaps, No. 2,	129
Albion Cake,	118	Cookies, No. 1,	129
Cake Filling,	118	Marshmallow Cookies,	129
Walnut Filling for Cake,	118	Sugar Cookies,	129
Chocolate Filling,	118	Cookies, No. 2,	129
Cream Chocolate Filling,	118	Sour Cream Cookies,	130
Filling for Layer Cake,	119	Tart Crust,	130
Caramel Cake,	119	Love Knots,	130
Caramel Filling,	119	Cookies, No. 3,	130
Layer Cake, No. 2,	119	Crullers, No. 1,	130
Snow Cake,	119	Crullers, No. 2,	130
Cold Water Cake,	120	Crullers, No. 3,	131
Pearl Cake,	120	Crullers, No. 4,	131
Layer Cake, No. 3,	120	Nut Crackers,	131
White Fruit Cake,	120	Brambles,	131
Lemon Cake, No 2,	120	PICKLES.	
Rolled Jelly Cake, No. 1,	121	Higdon, Pickles,	133
" " " No. 2,	121	Piccalilli,	133
Queen Cake,	121	Spiced currants,	133

INDEX—HATFIELD COOK BOOK.

	PAGE
French Chow Chow,	134
Grape Catsup,	134
Cold Catsup,	134
Sweet Pickled Peaches,	135
Chili Sauce,	135
Sweet Pickle, (citron,)	135
Mustard Pickle,	135
Pickle Lilly,	136
Piccalilli, (without cooking,)	136
Musk Melon Pickle,	136
Cucumber Pickles,	136
Onion Pickle,	137

PRESERVES AND JELLIES.

Preparing Fruit for Preserving,	139
Amount of Sugar to a Quart Jar,	140
Orange Marmalade,	140
Gooseberry Jam,	140
Currant Jelly,	141
Blackberry Preserves,	141
Lemon Jelly, No. 1,	141
Lemon Jelly, No. 2,	141
Quince Honey,	141
Green Grape Marmalade,	142
To Preserve Blackberries,	142
Buttercup Jelly,	142
Cider Jelly,	142
Cider Apple Sauce,	143
Orange Jelly,	143
Preserved Pears,	143
Currant Conserve,	143

BEVERAGES.

Beef Tea,	145
Beef Extract,	145
Raspberry Vinegar,	145
Red Raspberry Shrub,	145
Currant Shrub	146
Lemon Syrup,	146
Blackberry Cordial,	146
Mead,	146
Indian Meal Gruel,	146
Milk Porridge,	147
Soda Cream,	147
To Make Coffee,	147

	PAGE
To Make Coffee by Filtering,	147
To Make Tea,	147
Chocolate,	147

CONFECTIONERY.

French Vanilla Cream,	149
Orange Drops,	149
Fudge, No. 1,	149
" No. 2,	150
Peanut Taffy,	150
Walnut Cream,	150
Salted Peanuts,	150
Glaci Nuts,	151
Butter Scotch,	151
Fudge, No. 3,	151
Cream Taffy,	151
French Cream Candy Cooked,	151
Molasses Candy,	152
Chocolate Caramels,	152
Molasses, Taffy,	152
Peanut Candy,	152
Panochee Candy,	152
Salted Almonds,	153
Cocoanut, Cakes,	153
Nut Candy	153
Peppermints,	153

MISCELLANEOUS.

To Exterminate Red Ants,	155
Soda,	155
Remedy for Cough,	155
Laxative Fig Conserve,	155
Ham Brine,	156
Sausage,	156
Pickle for Ham,	156
Sand Bag for the Sick Room,	156
Japanese Cleansing Fluid,	156
Washing Fluid,	157
Poultice for Sore Throat,	157
Gloss Starch,	157

GEO. N. LUCIA,

We make a specialty of

Pictures and Frames

And carry in stock a large assortment.

Artists' Supplies, Stationery, Fancy Goods, Toys, Etc.

GEO. N. LUCIA,

229 MAIN STREET,   NORTHAMPTON.

B. E. Cook & Son,

Watches and Clocks,. .
Jewelry and Silverware,
Optical Goods. . . . .

112 Main Street,   Northampton, Mass.

FOR JEWELRY, OPTICAL GOODS,

STATIONERY, CAMERAS AND

CAMERA SUPPLIES,

CALL ON

F. W. ROBERTS,

27 Main Street,   Northampton, Mass.

HATFIELD, MASS.

J. H. HOWARD,

. . DEALER IN .

Choice Groceries, Crockery, Dry Goods, Boots, Shoes, Hardware, Etc.

Chase & Sanborn Teas and Coffees.

ARTHUR M. WARE,

Dealer in

Beef, Pork, Ham, Veal, Lamb, Provisions and Eggs.

52 MAPLE STREET,   FLORENCE, MASS.

Vegetables and Fruit of all kinds in their season.
A nice line of High Grade Canned Goods.

SPECIALTIES:—

Ware's Cooked and Pressed Meats, Boiled Ham, Sliced Dried Beef.

These goods are as good as I can make or buy. I sell them as reasonable, as I can, and do a satisfactory business.

TELEPHONE 119-5.

Londergan's King St. Market.

We have all kinds of fish, in their season, fresh every day.

WE HAVE THE EXPERIENCE OF SEVENTEEN YEARS, THE LONGEST OF ANYONE IN TOWN, TO AID US IN MAKING A SPECIALTY OF OBTAINING THE BEST GOODS POSSIBLE.

We have also a complete line of

Groceries, Fruits and Vegetables.

Give us a trial. Our team runs twice a week to all surrounding towns.

TELEPHONE CONNECTION.

WE BUY AND WE SELL ... FOR CASH ONLY!

No orders solicited.
No goods delivered.

WE CAN SELL GROCERIES TO THOSE HAVING THEIR OWN TEAM, JUST ONE PROFIT LOWER THAN OTHERS.

- - AND WE DO IT! - -

It pays to trade where you do not pay for delivering to some one else

ACME STORE,
CORNER MARKET AND WALNUT STREETS.

Good Cooking vs. Stylish Dress.

Good cooking will surely be promoted by use of the many excellent receipts printed in this book.

Stylish dress is just as surely promoted by frequent visits to the dry goods house of

J. E. LAMBIE & CO.,
NORTHAMPTON, - MASS.

THE LATEST NOVELTIES,

BOTH ORNAMENTAL AND PRACTICAL, AS WELL AS EMBROIDERY MATERIALS OF EVERY DESCRIPTION.

FANS, LACES, RIBBONS, GLOVES,

Can always be found at

E. P. COPELAND'S,

104 Main Street,   Northampton, Mass.

J. G. SMITH,

...DEALER IN...

Beef, Veal, Pork, Lamb, Poultry, Etc.

HATFIELD, MASS.

FOR A
FIRST CLASS ···**CARPENTER**···

CALL ON OUR TOWNSMAN,

EDGAR LYMAN,

Weather Strips a Specialty.

G. H. HARTWELL,

DEALER IN

Bread, Pies, Cakes, Crackers, Etc.

351 Bridge Street, Northampton, Mass.

Deuel's Stable,

NORTHAMPTON.

Teams of every description, with or without driver.
The best place in town to feed or hitch your horse.

FRANK D. DEUEL, Prop.
TELEPHONE 128-2.

MANDELL'S

IS A

GOOD PLACE

TO BUY

GOOD SHOES.

Mansion House Block, Northampton, Mass.

We sell Plants, Cut Flowers, Jardiniers and Ornamental Shrubbery.

Our prices are as low as it is possible to make them. Visitors are always welcome at our Green House.

FIELD, THE FLORIST,

Store, 279 Main St.,   Green=house, Cor. Prospect and Massasoit Sts.,

NORTHAMPTON, MASS.

M. Howes & Son,

Dry Goods, Groceries,

Boots and Shoes,
Hardware, Etc.

MAIN STREET,   WHATELY, MASS.

North Hatfield Store.

This is our first "ad" in a Cook Book. It is hard to write the right words, but we wish you to remember that we have all goods usually found in a country store.

W. B. McCLELLAN.

C. H. BOYDEN,

WHOLESALE AND RETAIL DEALER IN

Ice Cream, Fruit and Confectionery.

197 Main Street,

Northampton,   -   Mass.

Hardware, Farming Tools, =

SEEDS, BICYCLES, SPORTING GOODS,

GRAIN, FEED, LIME AND CEMENT.

J. A. SULLIVAN,

3 MAIN STREET,   **NORTHAMPTON, MASS.**

TELEPHONE 6-2.

❧ ESSENTIALS. ❧

FOOD!   HEAT!

With this Book and a "Richmond" Range you can make the best food on earth.

THE KELSEY HOT AIR GENERATOR

Is the Greatest Heater on Earth.

J. H. & W. H. RILEY,
RELIABLE PLUMBERS,

193 Main St.,   **Northampton, Mass.**

REFRIGERATORS,   ICE CREAM FREEZERS.

Kingsley's Sarsaparilla,
50 CENTS.

We wish everyone knew the actual worth of this preparation.

Other Sarsaparillas would have a small sale. That sounds large, but it's a fact. Try a bottle of it and you will say, as one man did in our store,—"I have tried three or four different makes of Sarsaparilla, but yours takes right hold. It seems to be all medicine."

We make this Sarsaparilla and refund your money if you do not find it at the least, the equal of any dollar Sarsaparilla.

People who have tried it say it is the best one made.

CHAS. B. KINGSLEY,
Prescription Druggist,

140 Main Street,   **Northampton.**

A GOOD COOK USES THE BEST FLOUR.

Pillsbury's Best and White Lily

Are Still at the Head.

Commercial Fertilizers

For All Crops.

WOOD AND LIME ASHES.

All kinds of

.. FEED ..

always on hand.

POULTRY FOOD THAT WILL MAKE HENS LAY WHEN EGGS ARE HIGH.

MOWING MACHINES, TEDDERS, HORSE RAKES WEEDERS, CULTIVATORS,
and all other

Agricultural Implements.

S. & H. A. WILDER,
North Hatfield, Mass.

CHAS. R. FITTS,

Furniture, Carpets and Draperies.

FURNISHING UNDERTAKER.

Northampton, Mass.

.. NOVELTIES ..

IN

Ladies' Neckwear and Infants' Goods

AT

E. C. POMEROY'S,

122 Main Street,   Northampton, Mass.

A. G. FEARING,

Northampton, Mass.

Dry Goods, Notions and Carpets.

All at the Lowest Cash Prices.
No fictitious quotations allowed in this store.
We show goods with pleasure.

YOU WILL FIND

EVERYTHING

IN THE

...DRUG LINE...

AT

COBURN & GRAVES,

OPP. COURT HOUSE, NORTHAMPTON, MASS.

WHEN IN WANT OF THE BEST

TEAS AND COFFEES
OR CHOICE GROCERIES,

FRUITS AND VEGETABLES IN THEIR SEASON,

GO TO

K. H. STONE'S GROCERY,

28 Main Street, Northampton.

For Watches, Clocks, Jewelry. Silverware,
Spectacles or Eye Glasses.

..TRY..

C. H. GOULD,

153 Main Street, Northampton, Mass.

Expert Watch Repairer.
Satisfaction Guaranteed.

INSURANCE,

REAL ESTATE,

INVESTMENTS.

NOTARY PUBLIC.

All business pertaining to Estates and Trusts carefully managed.

. . OUR SHOES . .

*ARE WHAT WE REPRESENT
THEM TO BE,*

The Best for the Price, that Money Can Buy.

F. H. DRURY & CO.,

Northampton, Mass.

FORBES & WALLACE,
SPRINGFIELD, 1899.

DAD:—

You know Forbes & Wallace's store in Springfield! You know you can get almost everything there! You know that prices are generally lower there than elsewhere for the same articles! Do you also know that they take anything back which you buy of them and do not find satisfactory? Do you know that they advertise:—

"Your money back, if when you get home you'd rather have it than what you got for it"?

FORBES & WALLACE,
Main, Vernon and Pynchon Streets,
Springfield, Mass.

Hatfield Cook Book.

Copies of this valuable Cook Book containing tested Receipts may be had from members of
"*REAL FOLKS*,"
Hatfield,
Hampshire Co. *Mass.*

www.ingramcontent.com/pod-product-compliance
Lightning Source LLC
Chambersburg PA
CBHW031447160426
43195CB00010BB/882